Robert I

Mary Shelley

and the Birth of Frankenstein

Illustrated by

Cheryl Ives

First published in 2009

Stone Publishing House
17 Stone House
North Foreland Road
Broadstairs
Kent CT10 3NT

www.stonepublishinghouse.com

ISBN: 978-0-9549909-2-3

Typeset in 12pt Garamond by Troubador Publishing Ltd, Leicester, UK
Printed in Great Britain by TJ International, Padstow, Cornwall

Contents

VOLUME 1
Before Frankenstein 1

VOLUME 2
Frankenstein 43

VOLUME 3
After Shelley 103

VOLUME ONE

Before Frankenstein

Chapter 1

England, 30th August 1797

Storms continued to sweep the country. They had been doing so since the middle of July. Not even the oldest inhabitant could remember anything like it. Sudden flashes of lightning caused horses to rear up in the streets, spilling bags and cases from the tops of carriages. Distant rumbles of thunder grew louder and louder until they boomed and crackled directly overhead, terrifying not just children but adults too. A few heartbeats of silence. Then the rain began. Cold, punishing, rain.

In Somers Town, London, Mary Wollstonecraft went into labour. Believing that only women should be present at a birth, she asked her husband, William Godwin, to send for a midwife. With the arrival of Mrs Blenkinsop, who was the matron at the New Westminster Lying-In Hospital in Lambeth, Mary felt she was in safe hands and asked William to leave her. As he set foot outside the rain had begun to ease. The sky was murky but he could make out a strange shape – a flare of light with a mysterious tail. He recognized it immediately. A comet. This was surely a hopeful sign for them.

The couple were hoping to have a boy, and were ready to name him William. But, as the storm continued, on Wednesday 30th August at 11.20 p.m. she gave birth to a daughter, Mary.

There was a further problem. The afterbirth, or placenta, which is usually expelled a few minutes after the delivery, failed to appear. So Mrs Blenkinsop sent for an obstetrician from the same Hospital, a Dr Poignard, to come to remove it by hand. It was a painful and bloody process that took eight hours, and left the mother very weak and needing round the clock attention. Dr Poignard sent for two doctors, a nurse and an old friend, Dr Fordyce, to look after her.

When she regained some of her strength, friends started to visit her again, and baby Mary was brought to her to be fed. But three days later, on Sunday 3rd September, she fell ill and began shivering fits. Some of these fits were so violent that her husband in the room below said that he could hear the floorboards rattling. Fearing that she would infect her baby, Dr

Fordyce forbade her to feed little Mary any longer and brought in puppy dogs to suck off the milk.

Without realizing it, Dr Poignard had introduced infection into Mary's body, and she was suffering from septicaemia. Doctors at this time knew nothing about the causes of infection, and so did not sterilize their hands or their instruments. With no antibiotics available, the infection spread quickly to her lungs, kidneys and brain. Every effort was made to save her, but to no avail. Within ten days Mary Wollstonecraft was dead. She was just thirty-eight years old. Her husband recorded in his diary for Sunday 10th September only four words: '20 minutes before 8.'

Chapter 2

Baby Mary was taken to a family friend, a Mrs Maria Reveley, so that her father could have some time on his own to grieve. William was unable to speak about the loss of his wife. In a letter to a friend he had once said: 'I firmly believe that there does not exist her equal in the world. I know from experience we were formed to make each other happy.' Before she died Mary Wollstonecraft had whispered that Godwin was 'the kindest, best man in the world.'

In days before photographs, people had to find other mementoes to remind themselves of their loved ones. During her pregnancy William had already commissioned John Opie to paint a portrait of his wife. Now he had a death mask made of her, and tresses of her hair cut as keepsakes.

On 15th September Mary Wollstonecraft was buried in Old St Pancras Churchyard. William was too upset to be able to attend.

Young Mary's parents were exceptional people – both well-known for their writing. She was determined that, when she grew up, she too would be a writer. Her father had written a book of philosophy called *Political Justice*, and a novel called *Caleb Williams* – the first detective thriller written in English. William Godwin was a man who rarely showed any emotion, though when he was under stress he suffered from fainting fits, his skin flared up and his long nose became inflamed. It was a nose that Mary was to inherit. He looked down this nose at the monarchy and organized religion, both of which he wanted to abolish – as the Revolutionaries had recently done in France. He, too, had radical views – he was against private ownership, and lived according to this principle by owning no property, just renting a couple of rooms in Somers Town (now Islington) in a building known as 'the Polygon,' because of its many sides. From there he tried to make a living by his writing.

Young Mary's mother was just as famous. Mary Wollstonecraft was also a radical who sympathized with the French Revolutionaries and cheered when they burnt down the Bastille prison in Paris. But it was as a feminist that she caused the greatest stir. Most women in her time were brought up to expect to marry, but Mary Wollstonecraft was not the slightest bit interested in that. She believed in free love and hated the idea of marriage which meant being a slave, a piece of property. She set down these ideas in her book *Vindication of the Rights of Women* which shocked opinion of the day and caused a whirlwind of abuse – not just from men but from women too. The well-known writer Horace Walpole called her a 'hyena in petticoats.'

When she met and fell in love with an American, Gilbert Imlay, she had no intention of marrying him. They lived in Paris during the bloodthirsty Reign of Terror, and in 1794 had a daughter, Frances, always known as Fanny. This caused a great scandal in a period when parents were expected to be married. Mary called Fanny her 'unfortunate girl.' But Imlay quickly got tired of Mary and started an affair with an actress. When he told Mary he wanted to end their relationship, she became depressed and tried to kill herself – twice: first with a dose of laudanum; then by putting stones into her pockets and throwing herself off Putney Bridge into the River Thames.

Soon after this she became friends with William Godwin; she had met him a few years before at a dinner party. They held similar beliefs. For a start, they both hated the idea of marriage: Godwin said that marriage was like being sentenced to hard labour. So, in August 1796, they became secret lovers, living in neighbouring houses and writing daily notes to one another. Only when Mary became pregnant did they reluctantly agree to marry, for the good of their baby rather than their own reputations. Within six months Mary Wollstonecraft was dead.

Chapter 3

When she was only nineteen days old, baby Mary's head was examined by her father's friend, William Nicholson, who was an amateur phrenologist. Phrenology had its origins in Ancient Greece but was now becoming very popular again. Those who believed in it claimed that the shape and size of a person's head revealed a lot about their abilities and personality. Having completed his examination, Nicholson's verdict was that Mary's head suggested 'considerable memory and intelligence.'

Godwin was happy to hear this but it did not make bringing up Fanny and Mary (his 'two poor animals') any easier. He did his best – he read to them, he took them to their mother's grave where Mary learned to spell from the letters on the gravestone; he took her out to play by the Fleet River; they went to the theatre, the shell grotto in Twickenham. Fanny, who was three years older than Mary, was especially a handful. In fact she was so noisy in the house that Godwin could not work. 'The poor children!' he wrote in a letter six weeks after his wife's death. 'I am myself totally unfitted to educate them.' When Mary had a fall, and when, soon afterwards, both girls went down with measles, it was the final straw. He decided that the only solution was to employ servants – a housekeeper and a nursemaid. The nursemaid taught Mary to read and write, using a book called *Ten Lessons* which Mary Wollstonecraft had written for Fanny. But the servants were either no good, or those who were good never lasted. He needed someone to care for the children. And soon William Godwin began thinking of marrying again. He proposed twice. First he asked the recently widowed Maria Reveley who had taken care of Mary when she was just a few days old. But it was far too early for her to think about marriage again so soon after her husband's death. His second proposal was to the author Hermione Lee who he met briefly in Bath. Again it failed – she found him too pushy.

It was then that one of his neighbours started to show an interest in him. She was a stout woman who called herself 'Mrs' Mary Clairmont, even though she had never married. She had two children – a five year-old son called Charles and a three year old daughter called Jane who was always giggling. Both were illegitimate and had different fathers, just as with Mary and Fanny.

One day when Godwin was out on his balcony taking the air, she called across to him: 'Is it possible that I behold the immortal Godwin?' He loved such flattery, and they soon became friends, taking their children on joint trips. They shared delicious picnics on Hampstead Heath, were amused by waxwork exhibitions and marvelled at displays of tightrope walking.

One of Godwin's friends, the poet Robert Southey, was shocked that he could marry again while a portrait of Mary Wollstonecraft still hung above the mantelpiece in his study. Several of his other friends thought that Mrs Godwin was a poor substitute for Mary Wollstonecraft. The author Charles Lamb called her 'a damn'd disagreeable woman.' Poor substitute or not, with a new wife it would mean that the girls would at least be taken care of, and Godwin could now concentrate on his writing. He agreed to see the girls for just half an hour each day when he rang the bell in his study at one o'clock.

Before they were married, Mrs Clairmont had managed to conceal some of her less pleasant personal habits. But as soon as they were married her bad temper was quick to show itself. She was constantly

complaining. She complained of living in London rather than in the country. She complained that before she met Godwin she had been used to living well. She complained that she never went on holiday.

Mary detested her stepmother who seemed to favour her own children above Fanny and herself. The very thought of 'Mrs G,' an 'odious' and 'filthy' woman, made her shudder. Her step-mother was also a very jealous woman. When visitors asked Mary to stand by the portrait of her mother and paid her compliments about their similarities, Mrs Clairmont simply could not contain her anger. At times she became so furious that she would rush out of the house, saying that she would never return.

So were sown the seeds of a deeply unpleasant and stormy relationship which ran its course, like a poison, not just through Mary's childhood but which would fester on well beyond into her adult years.

Chapter 4

When the family moved from the Polygon to No.41 Skinner Street in Holborn, William and his new wife had already started a book company. The business, which sold books to schools and to shops, was under Mrs Godwin's name. If they had used William Godwin's name – the name of a radical – it would have been doomed to fail.

The move had many disadvantages. Somers Town had watchmakers, goldsmiths and engravers who provided goods for wealthy customers; whereas in Holborn they were now surrounded by the slaughter houses of Smithfield and terrible poverty – dim, stinking alleys full of thieves and prostitutes, where typhoid fever was rampant. Being constantly chased by their creditors, the family could not afford to live in Somers Town any longer, and these premises were cheaper. Far better this than the debtors' prison.

Their new house was a five-storey corner building.

The bookshop and offices were on the ground floor where there was a curved display window for the books. The upper four storeys were for living in. The girls had a floor to themselves and a large schoolroom where they worked with their governess, Maria Smith, and where Mary could practise her large, loopy handwriting. From time to time, masters came to the house to teach the girls French and Italian, art, music and singing.

There would be other visitors. The clatter of iron wheels signalled the arrival of famous writers to tea and supper – the poets William Wordsworth and Samuel Taylor Coleridge, and the author Charles Lamb. [See pages 150-152]. Once, when they had been living in Somers Town, Coleridge had recited his poem *The Rime of the Ancient Mariner.* Mary and Jane had been hiding under the sofa to listen until Jane sneezed and gave the game away.

Mary loved to read – fiction, fairy tales and adventure stories. She also loved to scribble down stories of her own. One of these took the form of a funny poem about an Englishman travelling in France and not making himself clear because of his awful pronunciation. The poem, entitled *Mounseer Nongtonpaw*, was published by the family firm when she was only ten and a half years old.

Soon after she had completed it, Mary's left hand started to get very sore, and before she knew it hideous pimples, filled with pus, erupted all over it. Mrs Godwin called in a doctor, Dr Henry Cline, who put her hand in a sling and told her to open the pustules and apply a poultice several times a day. He also recommended the fashionable salt water therapy at a seaside resort.

So, leaving a rather put-out Fanny at home to look after the house, Mrs Godwin took Mary and her own two children to the seaside town of Ramsgate in Kent. The town's guide book confirms how seabathing 'has been found indispensably necessary, and indeed the only possible remedy in various diseases.' They stayed with Miss Caroline Petman who kept a girls' boarding school at No.92 in the High Street. In recent years the premises have become a shop called 'Nanny's Attic.' Every morning Mary took a ten minute walk down to the sands, hired a seabathing machine and took a sea dip. To her relief, the pustules soon began to heal.

But when, at Christmas, she went back to London her skin condition not only returned but grew worse, until it affected her whole arm. So Dr Cline prescribed another six months by the sea. This time her father sent Mary to Dundee on the north east coast of Scotland. He had a soft spot for the city which had

become famous for radical and revolutionary discussion. Mary would stay with friends of his, the Baxter family, who were happy to put her up without charging a penny.

The decision to send her away was not an easy one, as she was not yet fifteen years old. Her father took her to the wharf and stayed an hour on board the ship until it sailed. Fortunately, he was able to leave his daughter in the hands of a Mrs Nelson, who was travelling to Scotland to visit her sick husband. 'I daresay she will arrive more dead than alive, as she is extremely subject to sea-sickness,' he told Mrs Nelson. The voyage would probably last almost a week – it would depend on the strength of the wind.

The Baxters lived in a cottage overlooking the Tay estuary at Broughty Ferry, four miles east of Dundee. From her window Mary could see the Grampian Mountains, clad in snow. Each day, as she wandered along the beach and bathed in the sea, her health slowly improved, her arm healed, and her skin became bright and clear. She spent the time bathing, reading, writing stories and daydreaming. She saw whaling ships and expeditions leave for the Arctic. The Baxters took her to Edinburgh and St Andrews. Before long, they became her second family. Their son Robert who was seventeen fell in love with Mary and followed her to London when she returned. Their youngest daughter, Isabella ('Izy', as she always called her) who was four years older than Mary, became her first real friend. The problems of living in squalid Skinner Street with her awful stepmother seemed a long, long, way away.

After Mary had returned from a second visit to Dundee the following year, Fanny welcomed a young man into the house. The man, who had curly hair, wide eyes and a flushed face, had come to see her father. Having visited many times before, he was asked to make himself comfortable in the study. He had been sitting there for only a few minutes when the door opened just a fraction. A girl's voice called out softly 'Shelley!' The young man looked up and called out 'Mary!'

Chapter 5

It seemed that Percy Bysshe Shelley had always verged on the brink of madness. In fact his father had been advised to put him into a madhouse. He was already behaving in a peculiar way at his boarding school, Syon House Academy, where he blew up the playground fence and blew the lid off his desk. Known as Victor, he carried in his pockets such things as hard boiled eggs, chunks of bread and radishes. He also took around with him a tinder box (a lighter), and he loved to hold the flame until it started to burn his fingers. At home in the holidays he would hold hands with his sisters so that he could pass electricity through them. This impish sense of fun continued as a young man. Once he used a peashooter to fire a pellet at a waiter who dropped all his plates. Another time he changed the recipes of their cook by adding vile ingredients such as drops of human blood, part of a putrefied brain and mashed grave worms!

Shelley's family, who came from near Horsham in Sussex, was very wealthy and when he left Syon House could afford to send him to Eton, a top public school. There he experimented with magnifying glasses and chemicals. He burned holes in his clothes and the carpet, and electrified a tom cat. One day he stabbed a boy in the hand with a fork and was sent home with 'brain fever.' Known simply as 'Mad Shelley,' he was remembered for looking more like a girl in boys' clothing. But that suited him to the ground because he did not want to be like the rest of the world.

After leaving Eton he went to University College, Oxford. But it was too boring and old fashioned for him. So he chose to go his own way – skipping classes, reading alone for sixteen hours a day and wearing his hair longer than was fashionable. At night he did scientific experiments in his room. Amongst other chemicals, he sipped arsenic and nitric acid. His friend Thomas Jefferson Hogg remembers Shelley turning the handle of an electric generator until sparks shot out and his hair stood on end.

Shelley held several beliefs that were unacceptable to most people. For a start, he believed that governments should be abolished and that money should be distributed equally, as did William Godwin.

On the matter of marriage, he also held the same views as Mary's parents – he was appalled by it. Years later he wrote:

> I never was attached to that great sect
> Whose doctrine is that each one should select
> Out of the world a mistress or a friend,
> And all the rest, though fair and wise, commend
> To cold oblivion.

Shelley was an atheist, and with the help of his friend Hogg, wrote a pamphlet denying the existence of God. One of the lecturers at Oxford spotted it in the window of a local bookshop, passed it on to the college authorities, and Shelley and Hogg ended up getting expelled.

Now out in the world he had no need to work because his family could support him, and lend William Godwin money besides. So he had taken up writing poetry – poetry that was so moving that women were supposed to fall in love with him when they read it.

Shelley was now twenty-one. Mary was sixteen. She stood in the doorway of the study that afternoon wearing a tartan frock that she had bought in Scotland. She was slim, pale-skinned, with light, reddish-gold hair and lovely almond-shaped eyes beneath a high intellectual forehead. Her pretty smile and little sideways glances endeared her to him. In a letter to Hogg he wrote: 'The originality and loveliness of Mary's character was apparent to me from her very motions and tones of voice... I speedily conceived an ardent passion to possess this inestimable treasure.'

In fact, Shelley and Mary had met the year before at the Godwins. On that occasion Shelley had had his beautiful wife, Harriet, with him. Harriet had been just a sixteen year old schoolgirl when they had fallen in love and eloped to Edinburgh to get married. Shelley's father was so angry at the elopement that he had cut off his son's allowance. But the marriage had been an unhappy one. Shelley had quickly tired of Harriet, and her habit of reading books out aloud really got on his nerves. Being married to Harriet, he wrote, had 'felt as if a dead and living body had been linked together in loathsome and horrible communion.' For some months now they had been leading separate lives.

Shelley and Mary started going for long afternoon walks together in the grounds of Charterhouse School and in Old St Pancras Churchyard where her mother lay buried. All of these walks were chaperoned by Jane Clairmont because it really would not have been the done thing in those days for a young lady to have walked alone with a young gentleman, let alone a married man. The wife of the gardener at Charterhouse commented how 'the fair young lady and the young gentleman always retired to sit in the arbour and the little young lady used to walk up and down by herself.' All the while they told Jane, with a wink, that they were discussing metaphysics!

Soon they had pet names for one another. Mary was his 'Pecksie.' Shelley was her 'Elfin Knight.' He told her how his wife never loved him and had been unfaithful to him. On 26th June 1814 as twilight descended on Old St Pancras Churchyard they shared their feelings for one another. That night Mary wrote in her Journal: 'Shelley opened, at first with the confidence of friendship, and then with the ardour of love, his whole heart to me.'

Chapter 6

Events had certainly moved fast, for Mary had been back from Scotland for scarcely a month. In Shelley Mary saw everything that she had always wanted – a poet, young and handsome. He got on well with her father who was only too happy for Shelley to lend him money to help pay off his debts.

However, when Shelley told him that he planned to take Mary to live in Switzerland he lost his temper and banned Shelley from visiting again. He told his daughter that she must give him up and insisted that she write him a letter, which she did. But with the help of the bookshop porter, Shelley managed to smuggle a letter back to Mary.

Weeks passed. The two lovers were unable to see one another. Then, one afternoon, when Mary was in the schoolroom with Jane there was a terrible commotion downstairs. Suddenly, the door burst open and Shelley ran in, shoved Mrs Godwin out of the way and dashed straight over to Mary. 'They wish to separate us, my beloved; but Death shall unite us.' With a dramatic flourish he produced a little brown bottle of laudanum (a drug similar to opium) that he carried with him to relieve his aches and pains. 'By this you can escape from tyranny; and this (he took a small pistol from his pocket), shall reunite me to you.'

Jane screamed. Tears welled up in Mary's eyes. Several moments passed before she could speak: 'I won't take this laudanum; but if you will only be reasonable and calm, I will promise to be ever faithful to you.' These words seemed to calm Shelley and soon afterwards he left the house. All seemed to have settled down.

But a few days later the doorbell rang at midnight. On the doorstep stood a man from the inn where Shelley was staying. The man said that Shelley had taken a dose of laudanum and that he was walking up and down in a most peculiar fashion.

Next morning a letter arrived from Shelley saying that unless Mary joined him he would kill himself. Mary took these threats seriously. So, ignoring the warnings from her father, she agreed to run away with Shelley. They would go to France and from there to Switzerland - and freedom.

At four o'clock in the morning on 28th July 1814

Shelley's carriage parked on the corner of Holborn and Hatton Garden, waiting for Mary to appear. Jane begged to go with them. Mary was happy to have her as a companion; besides, Jane had made excellent progress at learning French and might prove useful.

And so, as quietly as they possibly could, the two girls finished their packing and put on their black silk travelling dresses and bonnets. At a couple of minutes before four o'clock Mary crept downstairs, left a letter on her father's dressing table, then ran as fast as she could to Shelley's carriage. A few words were exchanged. Shelley agreed to take Jane as well. Mary ran back to fetch her and help with her baggage.

The driver whipped the horses. Mary gave Shelley one of her little sideways glances and smiled. 'She was in my arms,' wrote Shelley. 'We were safe!'

Chapter 7

As dawn broke they reached the port town of Dartford along the Thames estuary. The constant jolting of the carriage had made Mary travel sick and she was glad of a rest. But Shelley was worried about losing time. He was convinced that they were being followed and that if they stopped their pursuers would catch them up. Even with the aid of fresh horses the journey to the coast took another eleven hours in sweltering temperatures.

At four o'clock that afternoon they reached Dover. Mary had a swim to revive herself while Shelley went off to hire a sailing boat. By six o'clock they had set sail for France. Progress was slow as there was so little wind. Then came a squall, thunder and lightning. Mary was violently seasick. Shelley expected the worst and prepared to die. But after a while the storm eased and the sailors took advantage of a northwest wind that took them to Calais. There they rented rooms in

Dessein's Hotel and started to keep a journal in a green notebook. Shelley made the first entry: 'Mary was there.' Mary added: 'Shelley was also with me.'

The next evening they were told that 'a fat lady' with a big bottom had arrived. It was Mrs Godwin, who was accusing them of taking her daughter away. She made Jane listen all night to arguments about why she must come back to London with her. But in the end Shelley persuaded Jane to stay and Mrs Godwin was forced to return alone. From about that time, so as to mark a clear break in her life and the beginning of her freedom, Jane began to call herself Claire.

From Calais they travelled in a two wheeled carriage called a cabriolet to Paris, where they walked in the Tuileries Gardens and went to Le Procope, the oldest café in Paris, once frequented by the famous writers Voltaire and Rousseau. Prices in the city were expensive and their money soon began to run out. Shelley sold his watch and chain but he knew they would surely have to borrow money if they were ever to get to Switzerland. To make the little money they did have last as long as possible they decided to walk – even though it was about two hundred and fifty miles! They bought a donkey to carry their luggage but in spite of the owner's promises it was not up to the job so they traded it in for a stronger mule. In all this switching around Mary's trunk with all her letters and writing was left behind.

About a hundred miles into their journey Shelley sprained his ankle. So they decided to sell the mule and buy a cart in which to complete the journey. This added expense meant that they could only afford to stay in the cheapest inns. Mary complained about how dirty they were, and Claire said that the rats kept her awake, that she could feel their cold paws on her face.

As they drew near the border with Switzerland, Shelley teased Mary by suggesting that she bathe naked in a stream. He even offered to gather leaves to dry her. There was little chance of being seen from the road as bushes surrounded the stream. When Mary refused the dare Claire sided with Shelley and began to taunt Mary for her lack of courage. How dare she, thought Mary. If it was not for their kindness in agreeing to take her with them, Claire would still be back in smoky Holborn.

Slowly they headed towards the Swiss Alps which were rumoured to be infested with monsters and dragons; but all they encountered was a baby squirrel that promptly bit Mary's finger. On 19th August they reached Neuchâtel. They hoped beyond hope that money would be awaiting them from home. But no such luck. The following day, however, Shelley managed to borrow some money from a banker. This meant they could afford to rent rooms, which they did, in a house at Brunnen on Lake Lucerne. Mary was delighted with the spot. She loved the lake, the mountains and the wild forests: 'I feel as happy as a new-fledged bird, and hardly care what twig I fly to, so that I may try my new-found wings.'

The couple soon developed a daily routine. In the morning they read and wrote separately. They would have lunch together at midday. In the afternoon they would go sightseeing, run errands, and Mary would do housework. In the evening they would read together.

To the locals they were the objects of considerable interest, not to mention scandal. They had heard that Mary and Shelley had run away. Rumour had it that the impoverished William Godwin had sold Mary to Shelley for £800 and Claire for £700. An inquisitive Swiss gentleman asked Claire to her face whether she, like Mary, had run away for the sake of love. 'Oh! Dear no!' she replied with one of her giggles. 'I came to speak French.'

Chapter 8

Shelley often felt home-sick. He would complain of knowing no-one and dreamed of living in a 'fixed, settled, eternal home.' For him, Windsor, on the banks of the Thames and close to London, would be perfection.

Mary, on the other hand, loved being away from England where she found life dull and restrictive and the people conventional, full of morals. She had inherited her enthusiasm for travel from her mother who had toured Sweden, Norway and Denmark. Her travels were also something which she could write about with confidence, and when Mary returned she published an account of their travels as *History of a Six Weeks Tour*.

But to stay any longer abroad they needed money. As it was, they were almost penniless. They had no option but to start their long journey back home, travelling the cheapest route possible, by boat along the River Rhine.

On 13th September they docked in Gravesend, Kent, tired and dishevelled. Shelley did not even have the nine guineas he needed to pay for their fare, and had to persuade the captain to let him disembark and go to London to collect the money. Although he managed to get enough for their fare, he found it impossible to raise a loan. First he tried Mary's father, but he refused to see them. As far as William Godwin was concerned, his daughter was guilty of a crime: she had broken up Shelley's marriage with Harriet. So they tried to get money from Shelley's banker – not a halfpenny; his publisher – no chance; his friends – hopeless. The only course of action left was to approach Harriet. For two long hours he left Mary in the carriage with Claire until he managed to persuade his wife to lend him some. With Harriet's money, Shelley and Mary were able to put themselves up in a hotel for a few days.

Harriet still loved him and no doubt hoped Shelley would return to her. But two weeks later, just as Harriet was on the verge of giving birth to a son, he wrote her a letter, telling her: 'I am united to another. You are no longer my wife.' He went on to wish her well, and asked her to send him some stockings, handkerchiefs and books!

Chapter 9

Shelley was certain that his pursuers were everywhere – spying on him, chasing him with sticks, ready to shoot at him through the curtains. He called them 'men dressed in black.' So, while Mary and Claire rented lodgings, Shelley went into hiding. Only on Sundays could he safely show his face in London because on that day bailiffs did not work and he could not be arrested for debt. At other times he took a risk, as did Mary, and they managed to meet in secret in one of the capital's many coffee houses. 'You may meet me with perfect safety at Adams's, No.60 Fleet Street' he told her. 'I shall be in the shop precisely at 12 o'clock.' Once he had to pawn his microscope so that he could afford to buy them dinner.

They dreamed up ways to get out of their difficulties – they called it their "running-away" scheme. Perhaps they could set up a little colony in the west of Ireland.

By 9th November Shelley had succeeded in raising a loan. He was, after all, heir to a fortune, and would pay the money back when his grandfather died. He wrote to Mary: 'My dearest, best love, only one day more, and we meet... I find that I have no personal interest in any human being but you, and you I love with my whole nature.'

On the following morning Mary, Shelley and Claire moved into rooms in Nelson Square. Although together again, things were far from ideal. Mary was often unwell with morning sickness and confined to bed; but rather than stay with her, Shelley often went on jaunts with Claire. Meanwhile, Mary grew close to Shelley's college friend, Thomas Hogg. When Shelley had introduced Mary to Hogg he had instantly fallen in love with her. This did not bother Shelley in the slightest because he believed in free love. Soon Hogg was visiting Mary every evening and sometimes staying all night. On New Year's Day 1815 Hogg told Mary that he loved her. Mary replied that she was fond of him, but it would always be Shelley that she loved.

On 22nd February Mary gave birth to a baby girl who they named Clara, out of loyalty to Claire. The baby was two months early and the doctor gave no hope of her surviving. But Mary was unwilling to accept what he said and refused to take the infant away from her breast. To everyone's surprise she began to suckle, and the doctor said that perhaps there was some hope after all for the baby. When he heard this, Shelley went out and bought a cradle.

On the eleventh night, in more comfortable lodgings further down the street, the baby seemed to be sleeping soundly and so Mary did not wake her to suckle. But next morning, when she went to feed her, she found her baby dead, her body all twisted and lifeless.

Mary would never forget the death of Clara: 'Stay at home… think of my little dead baby,' she wrote in her Journal on 12th March 1815. 'This is foolish, I suppose; yet whenever I am left alone to my own thoughts, and do not read to divert them, they always come back to the same point – that I was a mother, and am so no longer.' She dreamed about Clara night after night, 'that my little baby came to life again, that it had only been cold and that we rubbed it by the fire and it lived…' Her own mother, Mary Wollstonecraft, had died as a result of giving birth to her. Now she had let her own baby die.

VOLUME TWO

Frankenstein

Chapter 10

They moved to Windsor, as Shelley had always planned, and lived near Windsor Great Park in an isolated brick cottage with a garden. The cottage, said Shelley, was so secluded that even the tax-collector did not know it! Mary chose a room for her study and settled down to her usual schedule of work in the morning and relaxation in the afternoon. On bright days they would read under the trees in the park. They had never been more settled.

The only thing which spoilt it was Shelley's poor health. A doctor diagnosed abscesses on his lungs, while a friend blamed the condition on the Shelleys' vegetarian and teetotal diet, and in particular Percy's obsession with green tea, lemonade and bread and butter. (His favourite dish was bread soaked in hot water and sprinkled with nutmeg). Half the time he was so lost in his books and thoughts that he could not remember whether he had eaten or not. As Ann Wroe has written in a recent biography of Shelley, his was the world of a poet 'into which earthly life keeps intruding.'

He had little time for Mary, who was now pregnant again and causing something of a sensation by wearing loose clothes and refusing to lace herself up. On 24th January 1816 she gave birth to a son who they named William, after Mary's father. Perhaps it was an attempt to patch their quarrel up. If so, it did not work, and father and daughter continued to ignore one another if they passed in the street on her visits to London.

Envious of Mary's success in bearing a healthy son to a well-known poet, Claire was determined to capture her own poet. She set her heart on Lord Byron, the most famous writer of the day, and, like Shelley, also married. Byron (or Albe, as he was known) was renowned for his handsome looks – his dark, curly hair and penetrating blue-grey eyes. He was also notorious for his outrageous behaviour. It was said that he used a human skull as a drinking cup. As a student at Trinity College, Cambridge, he kept a pet bear. Now a young man, he owned a menagerie that included peacocks and geese, a crane, a fox, monkeys, a badger, a crocodile and a dog called Boatswain. Byron was still more renowned for his sex life, and no chambermaid was supposed to be safe in the inns where he stayed. There were also allegations of incest, of a child he had conceived by his sister, Augusta. Another of his conquests, the novelist Lady Caroline Lamb, wife of the prime minister, summed him up as 'mad, bad and dangerous to know.' Certainly, as far as his fellow-lords were concerned, he was an embarrassment, and they were relieved that he took frequent breaks abroad.

For Byron, marriage and children were simply encumbrances that tied him down and hemmed him in. Indeed, after the birth of their daughter, Ada, he had sent his wife away with their baby. For Claire, there was no prospect of any long term relationship with him. But that did not bother her in the slightest. For her, the present was all that mattered.

That winter, Claire wrote a letter to Byron introducing herself, saying how she knew the daughter of Mary Wollstonecraft and William Godwin. Byron was intrigued and towards the end of April she had arranged a secret meeting with him at his mansion in Piccadilly. Byron was supposed to have had a desk crammed with letters from all sorts of love-smitten women, such as Claire! Soon afterwards they became lovers. Before long Claire became pregnant.

Leaving poor Fanny behind in London, yet again, the four of them – Shelley, Mary, Claire and Byron – decided to spend that summer in the Swiss city of Geneva which had a reputation as a centre for free-thinkers. Byron would join them later, travelling in his own spacious carriage with his personal physician.

Storms lashed down on the travellers and their young baby as they experienced a terrifying journey by night through the mountains. Their carriage lurched and plunged in the pelting snow, and ten men were needed to hold it down and keep it on course.

When they reached Geneva, Shelley, Mary and Claire posed as husband, wife and sister so as to get rooms for a few nights in the Hôtel d'Angleterre. In the hotel register they described themselves as 'Atheist one and all.' Byron and his doctor, John Polidori (Byron called him Polly, or Polly Dolly) joined them two weeks later. Polidori was younger than his master but looked so similar that he was sometimes mistaken for Byron. He brought with him his books and his guitar.

The arrival of Byron's carriage created quite a commotion as it had a big crest with the letter 'B' on the side; and the interior included a library, a couch and a set of crockery so that he could study, rest and eat. Polly needed to help his master down from his carriage, as the poet had a club foot. Once inside the hotel, Byron wrote beside his name in the register that he was a hundred years old!

Mary, Shelley, young William and Claire rented a small house at Coligny, and hired a pretty young Swiss woman, Elise, as a nanny for William. The house was called the Châlet Chappuis and it had its own private harbour.

After a few days Byron joined them. The grand house that he rented, the Villa Diodati, had a terraced garden reaching to the Lake and a balcony overlooking the Jura mountains. The famous poet John Milton had once stayed there. Rumour quickly spread that Mary and Claire were sleeping with both Byron and Shelley, and the surrounding hotels are supposed to have rented out telescopes to their guests so that they could take a closer view of the scandalous little love nest. Some assumed that the tablecloths drying on the balcony were the girls' petticoats.

During the day, when Mary would stay at home reading, Shelley and Byron often spent their time sailing on the Lake. Shelley could not swim but what did he care? Like Byron, he believed in taking risks, in living dangerously: 'Let's not live to be old, Shelley.

Let the grim reaper take us in youth!' said Byron. Returning at dusk, they would spend the evening around the dying embers of the fire – talking about ghostly experiences, the possibility of immortality and ghoulish scientific experiments they had read about.

That summer, the summer of 1816, turned out to be the worst in living memory. It came to be nicknamed the 'Year without a summer' and 'Eighteen hundred and froze to death.' Some fifteen months earlier, in modern-day Indonesia, Mount Tambora, having snorted and snarled for quite a while, had finally erupted. Huge amounts of volcanic dust had been ejected into the atmosphere in a large column, twenty-seven miles high. It was the biggest volcanic blast to shake the world, and left behind it the largest crater ever known.

In the same way that today sea temperatures thousands of miles away in the Pacific Ocean, and jet streams and greenhouse gases have brought climate change to northern Europe in the form of torrential summer rain, so, in 1815, winds had begun to waft volcanic dust particles around the world.

The full consequences of the eruption were not felt in Europe until a year later, but when they did occur, they were to have devastating results. Paintings of the time show lurid red skies, full of dust. Little sunlight could penetrate through, and summer temperatures plummeted all over the world. In the USA and Canada summer frost and snow killed off crops. In Europe there were huge storms and hard, cold, endless rain. Major rivers, such as the Rhine, flooded. Throughout the year Hungary experienced brown snow and Italy red snow. The harvest failed and there were desperate shortages of food. Across Europe 200,000 people died of famine. In Britain and France there were food riots. Astrologers predicted the end of the world.

But it was in the Swiss Alps and valleys where the weather hit hardest. There it was colder than it had been for five hundred years. It snowed almost every week and the winter ice never melted. Grapes did not ripen, potatoes rotted in the ground. In the countryside the Swiss peasants made do by eating boiled grass and salt.

16th June 1816. Lake Geneva. The night was stormy. In the mountains lightning flashed from peak to peak. The wind roared. Thunder. Rain. Hail. It was midnight. While young William slept, Byron, Dr Polidori, Mary, Shelley and Claire sat in the drawing room of the Villa Diodati. Chandeliers hung from its high ceiling. A blazing log fire cast shadows over the dark furniture. Outside the French windows the storm raged. Trees were struck by lightning. They seemed to

come alive. Mary wrote: 'The lake was lit up – the pines on Jura made visible, and all the scene illuminated for an instant, when a pitchy blackness succeeded, and the thunder came in frightful bursts over our heads amid the darkness.'

Sitting close to the fire, they took it in turn to read from a book of ghost stories which Byron had bought from a bookseller in Geneva. It was now Mary's turn: 'On that fateful night I remember moonlight bathed the wind-swept shore which bordered our ancestral estate. Our daughter was late, very late, and I stood anxiously awaiting any sign of her return. I could see nothing. I could hear only the low moaning of the wind in the trees, a moaning that somehow drew my tired and nervous mind to a shape, hanging, twisted, like a discarded plaything from the hideous branches.' She passed the book to Claire: 'From a part of the grounds less dark than the rest I perceived a figure advancing towards the castle with slow and soundless deliberation, shrouded by a veil of mist that wreaked of the charnel house. Escape was impossible. We were trapped in his web without strength or knowledge to combat his dark and awesome power. The ghastly apparition entered the room. Paralysed with fear I watched helplessly as the spectre moved towards the bed. I felt suddenly icy cold.'

They all looked at each other for a few moments in silence. Then Byron laid down a challenge: 'We will each write a ghost story.' That night he started a tale about a vampire but gave up after a few pages. Shelley scribbled down a few lines of verse about one of his ghostly experiences. Dr Polidori, who at university had written a thesis about sleepwalking, had an idea of writing about a skull-headed lady who was punished for peeping through a keyhole. Strangely, Claire, who was used to sleepless nights, and had visions of giant spiders tearing at her body, did not come up with a story at all!

Only Mary took the challenge seriously. She had always wanted to do something 'great and good,' to be famous. For some women of her class, a career as a schoolteacher might be fine. But not for her. She wanted more. She wanted to become a famous writer. So she tried to think of a story. Not any old story but 'one which would speak to the mysterious fears of our nature, and awaken thrilling horror – one to make the reader dread to look round, to curdle the blood, and quicken the beatings of the heart.' Each morning her companions asked her 'Have you thought of a story?' Each morning she had to admit that she had not.

She thought back to conversations she had heard between Byron and Shelley – about the latest fascinating scientific experiments. She recalled how Dr Erasmus Darwin had managed to get a piece of vermicelli to move; how Luigi Galvani had made the muscles of a dead frog twitch by applying an electric current to them. Hadn't someone else made a decapitated dog kick its legs? So why not bring other forms of dead matter back to life by zapping them with electricity? 'Perhaps the component parts of a creature might be manufactured, brought together, and endued with vital warmth.' Think of the advantages it would have – to be able to live for ever.

Even today, two centuries after the time Mary was writing – when artificial limbs can be fitted; when a woman's eggs can be frozen for use in the future; when organs such as kidneys, hearts and livers are transplanted as a matter of routine; when synthetic chromosomes can be built from chemicals; and an animal-human embryo has been created so as to understand diseases better – the idea that a whole human body might be created is farfetched, unbelievable. It is true that in California a few people have left instructions that after death their bodies are to be frozen in liquid nitrogen, just in case future developments in medical science may bring them back to life again. But they are largely thought of as eccentrics: most people are extremely sceptical that

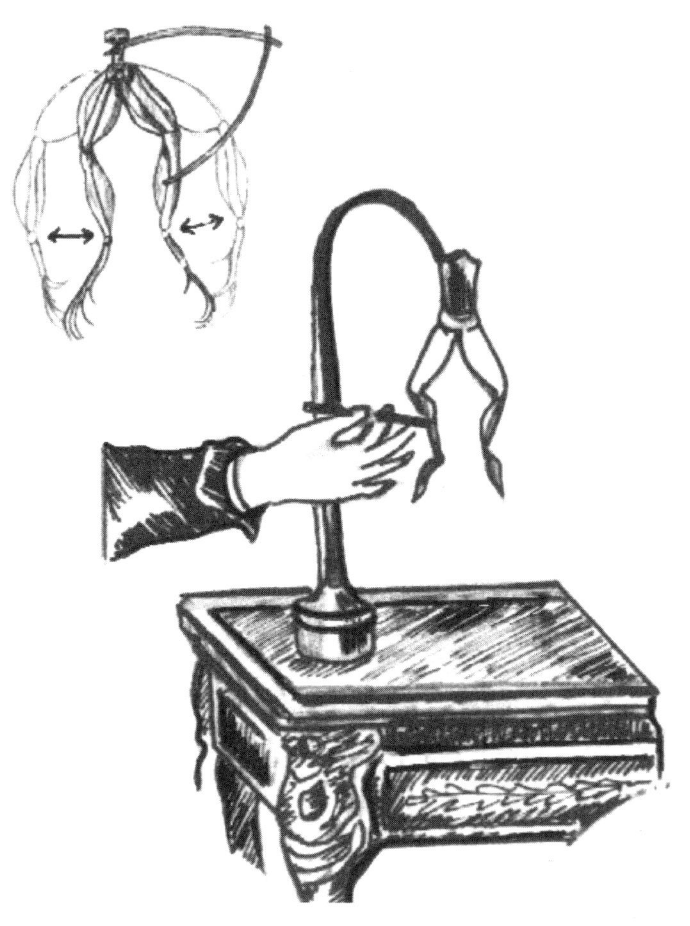

this will ever happen. Imagine, therefore, how much more amazing the idea of creating human life would have been in the early nineteenth century, even before the introduction of such basic medical techniques as anaesthetics and antiseptics, and being able to tell different blood groups apart. But that is precisely what she did. That night, when she put her head on the pillow she did not sleep:

'my imagination, unbidden, possessed and guided me… I saw – with shut eyes, but acute mental vision – I saw the pale student of unhallowed arts kneeling beside the thing he had put together. I saw the hideous phantasm of a man stretched out, and then, on the working of some powerful engine, show signs of life, and stir with an uneasy, half vital motion… He sleeps; but he is awakened; he opens his eyes; behold the horrid thing stands at his bedside, opening his curtains, and looking on him with yellow, watery, but speculative eyes. I opened mine in terror. The idea so possessed my mind that a thrill of fear ran through me.'

The next morning she announced that she had thought of a story!

Chapter 11

The hero of her story was Dr Victor Frankenstein, a lecturer from the University of Ingolstadt in Bavaria. He knew that he had it in him to give life to an animal as complex and wonderful as man: 'I will pioneer a new way, explore unknown powers, and unfold to the world the deepest mysteries of creation.' It made him dizzy to think about the possibilities. Perhaps, in time, he would be able to bring a dead body back to life. For now, his task would be to make a human being. He collected bones from dissecting rooms and slaughter houses. From these he planned to create a human being. So enthusiastic was he that he shut himself away in his laboratory – a solitary chamber, more like a cell, at the top of his house. Day and night he worked on his project, forgetting about family and friends.

Finally, the moment of creation:

'It was on a dreary night of November, that I beheld the accomplishment of my toils. With an anxiety that almost amounted to agony, I collected the instruments of life around me, that I might infuse a spark of being into the lifeless thing that lay at my feet. It was already one in the morning; the rain pattered dismally against the panes, and my candle was nearly burnt out, when, by the glimmer of the half-extinguished light, I saw the dull yellow eye of the creature open; it breathed hard, and a convulsive motion agitated its limbs.'

Dr Frankenstein had taken so much trouble, had worked so many hours. He had intended that the creature should be beautiful. But it was soon clear that something was very wrong:

'His yellow skin scarcely covered the work of muscles and arteries beneath; his hair was of a lustrous black, and flowing; his teeth of pearly whiteness; but these luxuriances only formed a more horrid contrast with his watery eyes, that seemed almost of the same colour as the dun-white sockets in which they were set, his shrivelled complexion and straight black lips... now that I had finished, the beauty of the dream vanished, and breathless horror and disgust filled my heart.'

Dr Frankenstein had created a wretch, a filthy demon, a monster – eight feet tall. He rushes out of his laboratory. Horrified by what he has made, he

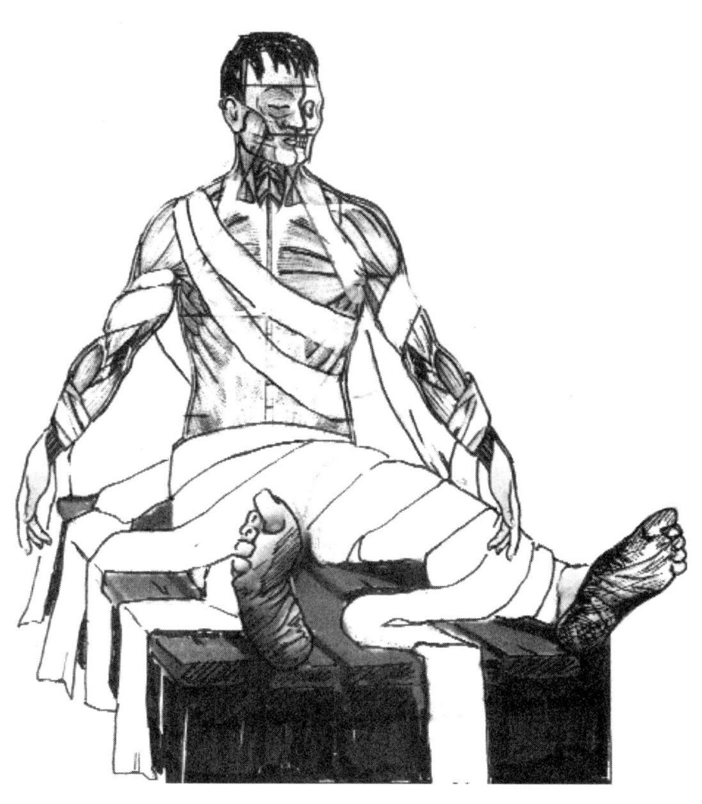

abandons the monster, suffers a nervous breakdown and has to be nursed back to health. No sooner than he recovered he receives a letter from his father telling him that his brother William has been murdered. He returns home immediately. In a thunderstorm near Geneva he catches sight of the monster again and suspects, rightly, that it had killed his brother. Instead, their servant Justine is blamed for the murder, found guilty and executed. By chance, Victor meets up with his creation again in the mountains. The monster admits to strangling William but promises to do no more harm, on condition that a female companion is created for him. Victor reluctantly agrees to the monster's request. But when the companion is nearly finished he has an awful premonition – she might produce children – and he tears her to pieces. The monster is furious, murders Frankenstein's best friend, Henry Clerval, and threatens that it will wreak further vengeance on Victor on his wedding night.

Frankenstein goes ahead and marries his cousin Elizabeth. Fearing the monster's terrible revenge, he sends his bride away to safety (or so he thinks) while he awaits the monster. But instead of the monster visiting him, it tracks down Elizabeth and strangles her in her bed. From that day onwards Victor devotes himself to only one task in life – the destruction of his creation. He follows him to the Arctic Ocean where the monster kills him. Full of remorse for what he has done the monster is determined to set himself on fire. As the story ends he sets off on a life-raft and is borne away by the waves.

Chapter 12

Mary, Shelley and Claire stayed in Switzerland, the birthplace of *Frankenstein*, until the autumn, when they returned to England. Claire was now six months pregnant. To avoid the Godwins finding out about Claire's pregnancy they found lodgings in Clifton, near Bath. When the baby was born it would be shipped off to Byron. With Shelley on business in London, Mary was left free to work in peace and quiet on *Frankenstein* – the novel that some years later he was to refer to as 'the fruits of my absence.'

Meanwhile, back in Skinner Street, London, Fanny had become desperately unhappy. She always felt excluded by Shelley, Mary and Claire, and she did not get on with Mary's father or his spiteful and abusive wife. She believed she was a burden on the family who were already short of money. So, she wrote to her aunts in Ireland to ask them whether she could stay with them for a while. But they refused to see her, perhaps believing that anyone who had grown up in Mary's household had somehow been 'contaminated' by her peculiar lifestyle.

On 9th October Fanny left home and went to Swansea in South Wales where she knew that it would be difficult to trace her. There she rented a room in the Mackworth Arms Inn, had a cup of tea and went up to her room. She asked that she should not be disturbed, saying that she was tired and would put her own candle out. This gave her the opportunity to take the overdose of laudanum which killed her. In a suicide note that was printed in the local newspaper, the *Cambrian*, she explained:

> I have long determined that the best thing I could do was to put an end to the existence of a being whose birth was unfortunate, and whose life has only been a series of pain to those persons who have hurt their health in endeavouring to promote her welfare...'

Mary's father tried to hush up the whole business. He told people that she had gone to her aunts Eliza and Everina in Dublin and had died from a bad chill. In a letter to Mary, his first to her since her elopement, he blamed Fanny's depression on his daughter's going off with Shelley.

Under pressure from his family to cover up her suicide, Shelley tore off Fanny's name at the bottom of the note so as to make it more difficult to identify her. In those days, to commit suicide was considered to be sinful, and suicides were generally buried in an unmarked grave by a crossroads. But the inquest jury were kind. Their verdict was simply 'found dead.' Neither the Shelleys nor the Godwins owned up to her identity and she was buried at the parish's expense.

Then came news of a second death. Less than two weeks later, when Mary was about half way through writing *Frankenstein*, she heard that Harriet Shelley had drowned herself in the Serpentine Lake in Hyde Park. She was in an advanced state of pregnancy. In her suicide note she wrote: 'I don't think I am made to inspire love, and you know my husband abandoned me.' Shelley was furious: her death is 'not to be attributed to me,' but to Harriet's 'beastly viper' of a sister, Eliza, who, he claimed, had driven her to suicide so that she would be their father's sole heir. Harriet's body was taken to the Fox and Bull Tavern where she was laid out with care. The jury's verdict, as with Fanny, was 'found dead' but unlike Fanny she was given a proper funeral by her father.

Chapter 13

Harriet's death meant that Mary and Shelley were now free to marry. In spite of their principles they, like Mary's parents, believed it was the right thing to do because they now had a child and there was another baby on the way. Furthermore, their family would surely increase in size as they expected to get custody of Shelley's two children by Harriet.

And so on 30th December 1816, in the presence of her family, Mary and Shelley were married at St Mildred's Church in Bread Street, London. Mary was now reconciled to her father. In Mary, Shelley had his ideal wife – 'one who can feel poetry and understand philosophy.'

They spent much of their time in London going to the opera with the journalist and poet Leigh Hunt and his wife, Marianne. Before long they became so friendly that they stopped addressing her as Mrs Shelley and started to call her Mary.

As Mary resumed writing *Frankenstein,* Claire's baby was born. Claire named the girl Alba after her father, Albe. She wrote letters to Byron practically every day (none of which Byron answered), describing their daughter's beautiful dark eyes and hair, that he would soon see her. It made her sad to think that one day she would have to part from her. Would he love their daughter and care for her as much as she did?

While Claire was resigned to having to give up her baby daughter, Shelley was determined to fight to cling on to the children he had fathered with Harriet. Plenty of people argued that he was 'unfit' and 'immoral,' an atheist who led a scandalous lifestyle. One even described him as 'an ignorant, silly, half-witted enthusiast, with intellect scarcely sufficient to keep him out of a madhouse, and morals that fitted him only for a brothel.'

After a court case that lasted almost two months it was decided that Shelley should lose all rights over his children, and they were placed in the hands of Dr Thomas Hume and his wife who were to act as guardians. The effect on Shelley was devastating and for a long time he was unable to write.

Instead he spent the time trying to find them a house, and in the middle of March Shelley found somewhere in Marlow, about thirty miles from

London. Albion House had a four acre garden, a large library and five bedrooms. But unlike their house at Windsor, this one was more on the beaten track, and soon after they had settled in his creditors finally caught up with him.

As spring blossomed, Mary completed *Frankenstein* and spent a week making corrections to the long sheets full of her large looping handwriting. Shelley helped with these corrections. In fact, he made almost five thousand edits. These changes were not always for the better, as he had a very wordy and flourishing style, more suited to poetry than prose. Some of the comments he made in the margin also show that he did not take his wife seriously as an author. But Mary allowed him to make the changes.

In days long before typewriters, let alone computers, Mary had to copy out the whole story neatly to show a publisher. Shelley also helped out here by copying the last thirteen pages. On 14th May she finished, and her 'hideous progeny' was ready to be born into the world.

Shelley presented the manuscript to Byron's publisher, John Murray. He said it was written by a very young friend of his who wanted to remain anonymous. Mary thought that this publisher was too old fashioned to accept such a story, and she was right, Murray turned it down.

The next publisher it was submitted to was Charles Ollier who sent it back by return of post! But in August it was accepted by Lackington which specialised in the occult. The publisher craftily wanted to keep all the profits of the first edition so as to cover the printing costs. Mary was in no condition to argue as by now she was almost ready to give birth. But Shelley managed to negotiate a contract for Mary to have one third of the profits. This piece of good news coincided with the birth of a baby daughter. She was named Clara Everina, in memory of her tiny baby who had died.

In January 1818 Lackington published five hundred copies of *Frankenstein.* It was subtitled *The Modern Prometheus*. In Greek legend Prometheus had stolen the fire from God and animated man out of clay. So, in *Frankenstein,* it is Man rather than God who holds the power to create life. The book came out in three volumes, and the anonymous author received £28. Many people thought that Shelley was behind the project. He had certainly written the Preface, and when he talked about 'his friend' the author, they assumed that he had written the whole book. This is an opinion that has survived to the present day. In her book *Shelley's Fiction* (1998), Phyllis Zimmerman argues that:

> '*Frankenstein* is a supremely poetic novel, but Mary Shelley was not a poetic writer. It contains complex symbolism, but she was a realistic author, not a symbolist. The novel alludes to a great deal of literature, some of which Mary Shelley had read, most of which she had not. Science interested Shelley greatly, Mary hardly at all. Gothic romance appealed to Shelley, but did not stimulate Mary noticeably. The French Revolution fascinated Shelley; it was not a subject of vital importance for Mary.'

John Lauritsen upholds this view in his recent book *The Man Who Wrote Frankenstein.* For him, the notion that the most famous work of English Romanticism, full of profound and radical ideas, could possibly have been written by 'an uneducated, teenaged girl,' is a myth. 'One expects the author of a literary masterpiece to be a great writer, which Shelley was and Mary most certainly was not.' His verdict is that Shelley wrote the whole of *Frankenstein* and for personal reasons chose to conceal his authorship. However, such a conclusion belittles Mary Shelley and fails to recognize her talents. She had received an education both at home and at school; she had written from an early age and had published a poem at ten years old; and she was fully conversant with the 'profound' and 'radical' ideas of her famous parents.

When *Frankenstein* was published, reviews were mixed. One said that the novel was 'a tissue of horrible and disgusting absurdity,' written by a madman and in the language of a madman. Many critics thought that the story was implausible, particularly the part where the monster manages to acquire his education by eaves-dropping at the door of a peasant's cottage. But others described the novel as sensational. Sir Walter Scott, while believing that it had been written by her husband, paid Mary the ultimate comment by saying that he preferred *Frankenstein* to any of his own romances.

During Mary's lifetime several editions of the novel were published, and revisions were made, partly to correct the grammar and the style. Of these editions, that of 1831 (costing five shillings) became the most famous. The revised edition of 1831 was the first to contain illustrations. Since that date the book has been translated into over two dozen languages, including Chinese, Japanese, Arabic, Czech, Turkish and Bengali.

Mary also explored the idea of restoring life in two short stories. In *Roger Dodsworth: The Re-animated Englishman* she brings back to life a man who had been buried in a glacier for more than a century and a half; and in *Valerius: the Reanimated Roman* a body is reborn without its soul.

Today, the film industry has made Frankenstein a household name. Set in a rugged castle, the films have managed to create a sinister and terrifying Gothic effect – by using eerie, swirling mists and dimly-lit rooms, with high ceilings and darkened windows. Over a hundred film versions of Frankenstein have appeared (a selection of which appear on pages 156-157). Although the 1994 film starring the British actor Kenneth Branagh keeps closest to the original book, it is the 1931 black and white version, with Boris Karloff as the monster, which is probably the most famous.

Frankenstein has also inspired cartoons and T.V. shows. Several episodes of *Flintstones* are devoted to 'Frankenstone.' ITV screened a modern version of Frankenstein in October 2007 in which Frankenstein had become a woman, Victoria Frankenstein, a scientist working on stem-cell biotechnology in a

BORIS KARLOFF
Frankenstein
COLIN CLIVE
MAE CLARKE
JOHN BOLES

medical laboratory in London, driven on by her son's organ failure. In January 2008 BBC TV aired *Frankenstein's Cat*, a show adapted from a picture book with the same name. It follows the exploits of Dr Frankenstein's experiment. The 'Frankenstein letters' appeared in an episode of ITV's detective series *Lewis* that was screened in February 2008. In these letters, all forgeries, Shelley gave Mary all the details of the plot which she needed to write her novel.

The reason for the continuing popularity of *Frankenstein*-related productions is doubtless because the power to create life remains a topic of endless fascination. It is also the subject of considerable ethical controversy. Is such experimentation the future of mankind? Or is it the work of the Devil?

Chapter 14

Spring 1819

Shelley was ill again. For some years he had believed that he was suffering from a fatal illness and would die young. At times he feared he had tuberculosis. More recently he had become convinced he had contracted elephantitis after sitting next to a woman with fat legs! His doctor prescribed a mild climate and a less hectic lifestyle. So Shelley and Mary decided to travel to Italy, taking with them Claire and the children – William, who was now two years old; Alba, fourteen months; and Clara Everina, who was now six months old. The little party was made up to eight by the presence of their Swiss nurse, Elise, and her young friend, Milly. They planned to explore the country as far as they could go – from Lake Como in the north to Naples in the south.

First they had to endure a slow and hazardous

journey across the Alps. Being atheists, they prayed not to God but to Napoleon Bonaparte who had succeeded in leading his soldiers across the Alps on campaign. Eventually they reached Milan from where, on 6th April, Mary wrote to Leigh and Marianne Hunt: 'We have at length arrived in Italy. After winding for several days through valleys and crossing mountains… we have arrived in this land of blue skies and pleasant fields. The fruit trees all in blossom and the fields green with the growing corn… Italy appears a far more civilized place than France – you see more signs of cultivation and work and you meet multitudes of peasants on the road – driving carts drawn by the most beautiful oxen I ever saw… The inns are infinitely better and the bread which is unbearable in France is here the finest and whitest in the world… In Italy we breathe a different air and everything is pleasant around us.'

On 7th May they arrived at Pisa but left after a couple of days because Mary could not bear the sight of criminals in chains mending the streets. 'You could get into no street but you heard the clanking of their chains,' she wrote. So they went on to Leghorn (Livorno), several miles down the coast, and spent a month there. Mary was not much more impressed with this place, calling it a 'stupid town.' But that did not matter because she had come to see the woman who had looked after her as a baby. Maria Reveley, who had snubbed her father's offer of marriage, had gone on to marry the poet John Gisborne – a peculiar looking man with a large nose, thin lips and a nasal voice. As they walked along the sea-wall they talked at length about her mother and father and their ideas. Maria Gisborne was a proficient linguist, a talented musician and a skilled artist. Oh to have had such a cultured woman as a stepmother, thought Mary!

From there they travelled inland to Florence but were told that dangerous fevers made it unsafe for them to stay – particularly for Shelley in his delicate condition. Instead they were recommended to go to Lucca where they settled in Casa Bertini. All, that is, apart from Alba, who was despatched with the nursemaid to her father in Venice where she would now be known as Allegra.

Lucca was a peaceful, idyllic spot, surrounded by mountains covered with thick chestnut woods and soothed by the rush of the river in the valley below. They were able to spend their time reading and taking walks in the cool of the evening. To make their life easier they employed a woman to clean and a man called Paolo to cook. Paolo cheated them 'through thick and thin' and they had to sack him. But their nursemaid Elise adored him, and much against Mary's advice, married him.

Mary would later come to write a novel *Valperga* about the life and adventures of Castruccio, Prince of Lucca. But for the moment she took the opportunity of drafting a letter to Sir Walter Scott, setting the record straight once and for all that she, and not her husband, had written *Frankenstein.* The only reason why it appeared anonymously, she said, was because she was so young and would not be taken seriously as an author.

The mild climate and peaceful way of life did Shelley's health a power of good and soon he was well enough to travel. They planned to go to Venice to visit Allegra. Much to Claire's dismay, she was no longer with Byron who had foisted her off on a couple called the Hoppners. But just as they were about to leave, baby Clara became ill. So Mary stayed with the children while Shelley and Claire went to Venice on their own.

After a while Shelley sent Mary a message to follow with William, Clara and the two nursemaids. The journey across Italy did her no good at all, and by the time they reached Este Clara had become very ill. Shelley himself was now suffering from food poisoning and in such a sour mood that he dismissed Clara's illness as no more than teething problems. Only when her condition worsened did he recommend seeing a doctor in Venice. Mary and the nursemaids succeeded in reaching Venice but did not manage to get to the doctor, only as far as an inn, outside which poor Clara died. She had been suffering from dysentery. Mary wrote a few years later: 'Venice [with] its stinking canals and dirty streets is enough to kill any child.'

Mary had had two baby daughters. Both she had called Clara. Both had died. During this period it was by no means unusual for children to die before they were five years old. Parents had to be prepared, stoical, ready to get on with life.

The couple had planned to tour Italy. What should they now do? Stay in Venice? But that could have been a death sentence for the lot of them. Return to England? But they had enemies there – after all, Shelley was considered so 'immoral' that his own children had had to be taken away from him. Besides, the climate in England had been making him ill and his doctor had recommended somewhere healthier.

So they decided to continue their tour of Italy. By the end of November they had reached Rome. From there to Naples the road was much more perilous, but they were consoled to be told that there had not been a robbery on the road for eight months. Of course, whether this was true or not there was no way of knowing. However, they were accompanied by a priest – a strong, muscular one – who would surely protect fellow travellers – even atheists! And it seemed they had good reason to have faith in the priest as they only witnessed one person stabbed to death on their entire journey. They reached Naples, but Shelley was too ill to complete the planned journey up Mount Vesuvius and they had to turn back to Rome.

Within days, William went down with what seemed like worms but developed into a fever. On 7th June he died. He was buried in the Protestant cemetery in Rome. It was the third child in succession that Mary had lost and she was still only twenty-one years old. His death had a devastating effect on her. 'After my William's death,' she wrote, 'this world seemed only a quicksand, sinking beneath my feet.' So great was the strain on her health that she was unable to continue with her Journal and she sunk into severe depression:

'We came to Italy thinking to do Shelley's health good – but the climate has destroyed my two children... to lose two only and lovely children in one year – to watch their dying moments... I feel I am not fit for anything and therefore not fit to live... I ought to have died on the 7th of June.'

Chapter 15

This part of Mary's life had been so full of tragedy that she called her diary the 'Journal of misfortunes.' When she resumed writing in it she had to start a new notebook. The entries show less confidence, a Mary who quickly became confused and felt foolish, frequently describing herself as 'a goose.' She is more irritable, forever moaning about being cheated and her friends not writing to her. She was also pregnant again, and she dreaded another cycle of 'hope, love and loss.'

Back home in England, protestors were gathering in Manchester, waving banners demanding 'Votes for All' – all men that is. Mary's mother had been one of the few people as yet to dare suggest that women too be given the vote. Mary and Shelley wished they could be there to support their cause, but they were almost a thousand miles away.

The couple began their return north from Rome towards Florence. They stopped again in Pisa, where to save money they stayed with Mrs Mason, a friend of Mary's mother. Shelley found Pisa 'humdrum' and 'a city of the dead.' Mary, on the other hand, found it a 'pretty town,' with red roofs, though she liked the Pisans themselves no more than on her previous visit. There were so many beggars, 'ragged-haired' and shirtless, and galley slaves in chains. The women wore dirty cotton gowns that trailed in the dirt. Their husbands strutted around as if they were lords with walking canes in their hands, but to Mary their bushy hair, large whiskers and pieces of coloured ribbon sticking out from their button holes made them look more like their coach drivers!

On 2nd October they moved to Florence and on 12th November Mary gave birth to a son. They called him Percy Florence. Shelley hoped that having a new baby would help lift Mary's depression. Not one bit of it because their money problems were worse than ever. The couple were so badly off that they even had to economize on baby clothes. And a few days later she was plunged into new depths of despair when she heard that her father had suffered a stroke. Even the arrival in Pisa of their friends Edward and Jane Williams did little to improve her state of mind.

Shelley wondered what on earth had happened to the bright-eyed enthusiastic creature he had seen that afternoon five years earlier in her father's house:

> 'My dearest Mary, wherefore hast thou gone,
> And left me in this dreary world alone?
> Thy form is here indeed – a lovely one –
> But thou art fled, gone down a dreary road.'

In the summer of 1820 he followed it with a cruel poem called 'The Serpent is Sent Out from Paradise.'

Mary's own writing reflected her darker thoughts. Her new short novel *Mathilda* focused on a young girl whose mother, just like her own, died giving birth to her. She, too, was sent to Scotland. When her father saw the manuscript the comparison was all too clear and he called it 'disgusting and detestable.'

Matters were made worse when Mary received a letter from Elise Foggi, whose husband they had sacked. Elise had always been a one for gossip. Her latest claim was that Claire was Shelley's mistress, that she had given birth to his daughter and 'disposed of' her in a house for orphans in Naples. It was certainly true that Claire and Shelley had gone to Venice together while Mary stayed behind in Lucca. But Mary refused to believe that Shelley had been unfaithful to her. It was far more likely that their servant had made the whole story up out of spite. They decided to move to Leghorn for a change of air and to think what they should do.

By the autumn of 1821 they had returned to Pisa where, for thirteen sequins a month, they rented part of a house along the River Arno next to the Palazzo Scotto. To the north-east they had a wonderful view of the surrounding countryside – vineyards, olive groves, mountains thick with pine woods, and were 'entirely out of the bustle and disagreeable puzzi [smells] etc of the town.' Shelley, who liked his own space and calm in which to work, occupied the top floor and Mary and Percy had the floor below. Shelley wrote 'there is plenty of space for the babe.' Soon afterwards the Williamses took an apartment on the lower floor of the house.

So as to complete the circle, Shelley encouraged Lord Byron to come to Pisa. He had already tried to get Byron to send his daughter, Allegra, to join her mother in Pisa but without success. Elise Foggi claimed that this was because Byron was trying to bring up his one year old daughter as his mistress! More plausibly, Byron was suspicious of the Shelleys' child rearing practices, knowing how they had recently lost two children at a young age. We know that he confided to a friend that by sending Allegra to Pisa he would 'look upon the child as going into a hospital' –

a fate at that time often resulting in a quick death.

But now Byron was ready to make a move. He asked Shelley to find him a 'large and magnificent house' in Pisa. Shelley leased for him the Palazzo Toscanelli which was the most splendid one available along the River Arno, and just a five minute stroll from the Shelleys' home on the opposite bank.

The house was large enough to contain a garrison and had dungeons below. According to Byron, it was so full of ghosts that his valet asked to change his room, and then refused to occupy his new room because there were even more ghosts there than in the first room. What was certain was that the house was full of servants, horses, dogs and monkeys, all of which Byron had brought with him.

When Leigh Hunt also moved to Pisa, the little colony of English writers, or 'Pisa Circle,' was now complete. Mary called them a 'little nest of singing birds' inhabiting a charming town. Even in November temperatures were so warm that fires were not needed, windows could be left open and they had to find shade from the burning sun.

Shelley's health seemed to improve. He took daily outdoor exercise, boat trips along the River Arno and practised shooting at pumpkins with Byron, who was the better shot. Feeling comfortable and at ease they settled there, believing that such an oasis of tranquillity could surely only help their literary careers flourish. Mary asked that tablecloths, napkins and notepaper be brought out from England. Also sealing wax, scissors, pencils, combs, a magnifying glass, and counters for Percy who was now two years old. Most important of all for Mary were her books: Homer, Rousseau, Horace. Her father had always encouraged her to have plenty of reference books around when she read, because 'to read one book without others beside you was mere child's work.' Then there was her writing desk. Inside was a diamond cross, a good luck talisman that might have protected the lives of her children in Italy. But despite request after request, the desk did not arrive for another two years.

Guests were invited to breakfast and dinner, and Mary took walks with them in the public garden and through the pine forests leading down to the sea. She also started to learn Greek. Greece had just achieved its independence from Turkey. Mary had heard about its beautiful islands which sounded like Paradise, and dreamed of going there some day with Shelley.

But Shelley had other ideas. By then he had met Emilia Viviani, a lovely nineteen year old girl with thick black curly hair. She told him how her mean stepmother had banished her to the Convent of Saint

Anna, tucked away in an obscure quarter of Pisa. There in winter she had to warm her hands in ashes and her only company was a caged lark to which she spoke and sang. Mary found Emilia a very silly and vain young girl, but Shelley found her very pretty and very clever too, and he quickly fell in love with her. Letting his romantic ideas get the better of him, he was determined to be her knight in shining armour and rescue her from the dark dungeons of this terrible 'prison.' He tried to persuade Mrs Mason who had put them up in Pisa, to help in his rescue attempt. His plan was for her to dress up as a man, go to the Convent and pretend that she was Emilia's boyfriend. But she would have nothing to do with it. As it turned out, all of Emilia's hard luck stories were a fabrication. In common with many other girls from wealthy families, she had been sent to one of the most exclusive boarding schools in Pisa until she was of marriageable age. In the meantime she would remain in the convent. Shelley was never to see her again.

Chapter 16

In April 1822 Claire was horrified to discover that Byron had taken Allegra out of the custody of her foster parents, the Hoppners, and put her into a convent in Bagnacavallo. The damp stone walls would make her ill. She had to be rescued. The Shelleys tried to calm her, reassuring her that Allegra would be looked after well in a convent, that the air in Bagnacavallo was the best in Italy. Better than in Pisa where both Shelley and Mary were starting to experience spells of sickness. Shelley was suffering from pains in his side which may have been kidney stones. To help relieve them, Mary and Jane Williams tried mesmerism. This involved trying to send him into a trance and suggesting that his pains will have gone when he came round.

Meanwhile, Mary herself was suffering from what she described as 'rheumatism in her head,' a kind of neuralgia which left her feeling low and listless. The arrival of their Cornish friend Edward Trelawny, with his tales of adventure and shipwrecks, did something to raise her spirits. But what Mary and Shelley both needed was a change of scene, a holiday.

And so, in the summer of 1822 the Shelleys, the Williamses and Claire Clairmont travelled north up the rugged coastline of the Cinque Terre to spend the summer at San Terenzo in the Bay of Lerici. Here Mary described the air as 'excellent,' the sea exceptionally blue and tide-less.

On an earlier visit they had picked out a lonely house close by the sea called the Casa Magni. Once it had been a boat house; it had since been converted to live in but was still more of a boat than a house. The ground floor was used for storage and the second floor had living rooms. There was a large central dining hall, from which Shelley's bedroom led off at the front to the left, Mary's to the right, and the Williams' behind. Skirting the whole length of the front of the house was a terrace that overhung the sea. In practice it was too small for both families and their servants, and this led to squabbling.

In spite of this, Shelley grew fond of the house and proudly told visitors arriving by sea to look out for 'the white house with arches.' But Mary hated the place. The wild revelry of the local fishermen every evening unnerved her. As for the house itself, it gave

her the creeps: 'The howling wind swept round our exposed house and the sea roared unintermittently' so that she always felt as if she was on board ship. She found it suffocating: 'I wish I could break my chains and leave this dungeon,' she wrote. But they seemed destined to be stuck there all summer.

A few days before they had left Pisa the Shelleys were told that Allegra had died from typhus. Seeing as Byron was living so close to them just across the river, they decided not to tell Claire out of fear she might take revenge. Now, two weeks later at San Terenzo she was told the awful news. Allegra was just four years old.

It was soon after this that strange things began to happen at Casa Magni. One evening, while on the terrace, Shelley saw a naked child rising out of the sea, smiling at him and clapping her hands. A few days later Jane said she saw Shelley pass by the window on the terrace twice in the same direction, even though he was not in the house at this time.

On 8th June Mary, who was three and a half months pregnant, started to bleed badly. In an effort to keep her conscious they gave her brandy and massaged her in vinegar and eau de cologne. But she continued to bleed heavily. In such an isolated spot there was no doctor who could easily be called. Shelley, in a flash of inspiration, filled the bath tub with ice and gently lowered Mary into it. The bleeding stopped. When a doctor eventually arrived, he told Shelley that his quick thinking had probably saved his wife's life but that she had lost the baby.

For the next fortnight Mary remained in bed, very weak and distressed. So weak, that when letters arrived from her father saying that they had been evicted from Skinner Street and begging them for money, Shelley intercepted them because he did not want to make Mary any more anxious.

And then Shelley's nightmares began. In the early hours he would rush into Mary's room screaming. He told her how Edward and Jane Williams had been in his room in a most horrible condition, scarcely able to walk. Their bodies had been torn to pieces, their bones were sticking through their skin. Their faces were pale, stained with blood.

'Get up, Shelley!' Edward had shouted. 'The sea is flooding the house! Mary has been strangled!'

The nightmares continued, night after night, with never a break.

Towards the end of June a letter arrived to say that Leigh and Marianne Hunt had just arrived in Leghorn. Shelley was keen to go and meet them. But Mary was still ill and tried to stop Shelley from going, crawling out of her bed on to the terrace where Shelley was looking out to sea. She clung to him, tortured by feelings that something awful was going to happen. But Shelley took no notice. On Wednesday 1st July he and Edward boarded their boat, the *Don Juan* (named after a poem that Byron had recently written in Pisa) and set sail for Leghorn.

Having met up with Leigh and Marianne Hunt, on Saturday they planned to return to Lerici but there was a storm, so they delayed. By Wednesday conditions were calm and fair again. In San Terenzo they watched out for their husbands from the terrace. But there was no sign of them. Nor on Thursday. Then a letter came from Leigh Hunt. It was addressed to Shelley. Mary trembled as she tore it open and read the words: 'Pray write to tell us how you got home, for they say that you had bad weather after you sailed and were anxious.' Mary dropped the letter. She feared the worst.

Chapter 17

Mary and Jane Williams lost no time in hiring a boat to take them to Lerici where they hired a carriage and headed for Pisa.

It was midnight when the two poor creatures arrived at Byron's palace. 'I looked more like a ghost than a woman,' wrote Mary later. 'My face was very white. I looked like marble.'

They hurried up a giant staircase and rushed through a large room over the hall. A surly-looking bulldog dozing outside the poet's room started to growl. Byron limped to the door, still fully dressed, as he was in the habit of going to bed late and sleeping until midday.

'Where is he?' she asked.

But Byron knew nothing.

The two women got back into their carriage and made for Leghorn where, exhausted, they slept for a few hours at an inn. At daybreak they met Trelawny who confirmed their worst fears – that Edward had been impatient to return to Lerici and that the *Don Juan* had set sail. A ship's boy called Charles Vivian had accompanied them.

There was still hope. Perhaps their boat had been blown towards the island of Corsica. They returned to Casa Magni with Trelawny, went out on the terrace and focused Shelley's telescope on every boat that passed along the coast. They combed the shore. Nothing. Mary took opium so she could sleep.

Next day Trelawny returned to Leghorn to see whether there was any news of them. When he failed to come back that afternoon it gave Mary hope. But at seven o'clock he returned. His face was grim. Mary took a step towards him, her hands outstretched. Jane collapsed into a chair. Gently, Trelawny told them the news they dreaded to hear, that he had seen the bodies of Shelley, Edward Williams and Charles Vivian. They had been washed up along the beach close to Viareggio. Edward's body had been discovered four and a half miles away, close to a hut used by soldiers patrolling the coast. Shelley's body had been found on the beach in front of the thick pinewood half a mile west of Viareggio's canal at a place called the 'two ditches.' They knew it was Shelley's body because of his thick, grey trousers, his white silk socks and the copy of some poems by his friend Keats who had died the previous year. Some witnesses said that a fishing boat had watched helplessly as they had sunk in a huge gust of wind at about four o'clock on Monday afternoon. Other witnesses said the vessel had deliberately run them down.

The next morning, 18th July, they set off with Percy to Viareggio. On the beach, close to the house owned by the Emperor Napoleon's sister, Paolina, were three white sticks that marked a temporary grave for the bodies. Mary wanted to take Shelley's body to Rome, to bury him next to that of their son William. The Protestant cemetery was so peaceful, Shelley had once said, that it 'might make one in love with death.'

But his body was in no fit state to be moved. Quarantine regulations meant that the bodies would be going nowhere and that only Shelley's ashes would find their way to Rome. In the meantime the bodies had to be covered with sand and quicklime to preserve them.

On 16th August, the bodies were exhumed. Very little was recognizable of Edward Williams. It might have been the carcass of a sheep as far as Mary could see. The flesh of Shelley's arms and face had also been eaten away. 'What is a human body?' she exclaimed. 'An old rag retains its form longer than he who wove it.'

After they had been formally identified, the bodies were cremated in an iron furnace exactly where they had been found on the beach. Leigh Hunt, Byron, some soldiers and a few local fishermen looked on as the fire burned furiously. 'He was too good for this world,' thought Byron. The great poet wanted to keep Shelley's skull – maybe he planned to drink from it - but it fell to pieces in the flames which could be seen from miles around. What remained of the back of Shelley's head rested on the red-hot bars of the furnace, and the brains bubbled and boiled as if they were in a cauldron. 'Don't do this to *me*,' Byron muttered, as he limped away. 'Leave my carcass to *rot*.'

Burning his hands as he did so, Trelawny gathered Shelley's ashes to take back to Mary, and fragments of bone for Claire Clairmont and himself – just as Mary's father had cut off tresses of his wife's hair as a keepsake. Some people in Viareggio shared a superstitious belief that if the ashes were taken to England the bodies could be resurrected.

For some reason one part would not burn. Tradition has it that it was Shelley's heart but many scientists today believe that it is more likely to have been his liver. Instead it only discharged a thick liquid. Trelawny gave the organ, whatever it was, to Leigh Hunt who took it away as a relic. Only when Jane

Williams wrote him a reproachful letter did he reluctantly pass it to Mary. Tearing a page from a book of poems to make an envelope, Mary placed his heart inside, and tied the small parcel with silk.

As for Shelley's ashes, they stayed for several months in the wine cellar of the British Consul before Trelawny took them to the Protestant cemetery in Rome as Shelley had wished. Mary wrote to Trelawny, asking him for details about the burial: Where exactly had the ashes been placed? What was the inscription on the tomb? Had he planted a cypress? She suggested that some neighbouring monks be paid to guard the grave. Trelawny wrote back to say that he had planted six young cypresses and four bay trees, and that these words had been inscribed on the tomb:

> 'Nothing of him doth fade
> But doth suffer a sea change
> Into something rich and strange.'

A few weeks later, the remains of Shelley's boat were brought ashore.

By then Mary had returned to the Casa Magni. A terrible sense of misfortune hung over the building like a thunder cloud. Behind the house, the beauty of the woods made her weep and shudder. She began to blame herself for all those times when she had been unkind to her husband. He had not deserved it. Really, his only defect had been to die too young. He was just twenty-nine years old. In an unpublished elegy Mary wrote:

> 'The Star of Love for me hath set
> And I must live yet not forget
> How once it shone upon my Brow
> Though I am lorn and lonely now.'

Shelley was gone – 'the sun of my existence, the animating spark of my life... I am deserted. A frightful vista of long drawn out years is before me.'

VOLUME THREE

After Shelley

Chapter 18

Shelley left Mary at twenty-four years old, a widow with a young son. Only two things now mattered to her – to give Percy a good education and to publish Shelley's writing. Believing that her husband had been misjudged by ignorant people, Mary was determined 'to make him beloved to all posterity,' transform him into a god, 'a superior being among men, a bright planetary spirit.' She was not interested in glorifying herself: 'For my own private satisfaction all I ask is obscurity.' It was an enormous task that she set herself, made all the more distressing when she came across references in his writing to her 'coldness' and to poems dedicated to Emilia Viviani, to Claire Clairmont, and to Jane Williams, praising her sweet singing.

But Mary was proud to be Shelley's widow. She would not swap her position with that of the most prosperous woman in the world. Certainly, she was short of money, and bringing up Percy was an expensive business. Although Shelley's father, Sir Timothy Shelley, agreed to help support his grandson, this support was conditional on Mary taking him to England and handing him over to a guardian of his choosing. This Mary could not bring herself to do: 'He is my all. My other children I have lost, and the pangs I endured when those events happened were so terrible... I could not live a day without my boy.'

She stayed for one year longer in Italy, 'dear Italy – murderess of those I love & all of my happiness.' After a period scraping a living by copying out some of Byron's poems to submit to a publisher, she decided it was time to return to England. With thirty pounds given her by Trelawny, she set off from Genoa to London on 25th July 1823 with Percy on her lap. They crossed the Alps in a slow, lumbering vehicle called a *vetturino,* and reached Paris, exhausted, on 12th August. She just had enough money to get them back to London, where they rented a dismal house in Brunswick Square. No more Italian sun. She now had to get used to London's 'infernal' climate – the dreary rain, the soaked pavements, the need to light a fire in September!

However, she was soon to make a wonderful discovery: *Frankenstein* had been made into not one but two stage plays. Today this could never possibly happen without the permission of the author and publisher, and substantial fees being exchanged for the rights. But in 1823 it was all perfectly legal. At the Lyceum Theatre was being staged *Presumption, or, The Fate of Frankenstein* by Richard Brinsley Peake; and at the Royal Coburg Theatre was *Frankenstein, or, Demon of Switzerland*, by Henry M. Milner. She went to watch the first of these with her father and Jane Williams. A number of changes had been made which set a trend for most, later, film versions. In the stage set a staircase leads up to Frankenstein's workshop, from which a glimmer of light is visible. A servant called Fritz – not in her novel - peeps through the window and runs off, terrified by what he has seen. The blue-bodied monster, or 'fiend' as Mary usually referred to him, throws open the laboratory door. Mary's monster had plenty to say, but Peake's monster only grunts. As it stumbles down the staircase the audience could see its hideous face, its black lips. Mary noted with satisfaction how the play 'appeared to excite a breathless eagerness in the audience.' In fact it was so successful that it was put on in New York in 1825. It was these plays that really got her novel known among the ordinary public.

A year later in London it was the turn of the parodies such as *Frank-in-Steam; or, The Modern Promise to Pay,'* and *Frankenstitch* who created his monster from the corpses of nine men using needle and thread. Since then there have been film parodies, notably Mel Brooks's *Young Frankenstein* or *Frankenstein Junior* (1974) with Marty Feldman. In the *Rocky Horror Picture Show* (1975) Tim Curry plays an alien from the planet Transexualvania called Frank-n-Furter.

Frankenstein was not just well known among theatre-goers. Even the Prime Minister in 1823, George Canning, had heard about him. He called Mary Shelley 'a child of genius.' She had fulfilled her ambition: she had become a famous writer!

The Godwins and their bookshop had moved to No.125, The Strand where Mary and Percy were given the attic to live in. After a long period apart, Mary and her bad-tempered stepmother were thrown together again. Mary hoped that their stay together would be only a temporary one. Even her father was not much better company. He had borrowed for the new business beyond his means to pay back, and his growing debts made him irritable. For many years now he had been relying on Shelley to lend him money. But Shelley was dead. He had no option other than to declare bankruptcy and sell M.J. Godwin & Co. Mary offered to help by promising him all the profits of her historical novel *Valperga.* But the book was nothing like as successful as *Frankenstein*, and only sold five hundred copies.

Undeterred, Mary had already started to plan a semi-autobiographical novel called *The Last Man,* about a sole survivor of the human race destroyed by plague in the 21st century. However, there was no prospect of it being published for several years to come. In the meantime she needed a dependable, regular source of income. So she began to write magazine articles. The first of these, 'Recollections of Italy' was published in *The London Magazine* in January 1824.

She met up with 'Izy' Baxter, her childhood friend from Scotland, and they caught up with all their news. But when they parted it was not long before the hours started to drag again. For, much as she loved Percy who was now five years old, she longed for adult conversation. But all she had was poor Jane Williams who had grown dreadfully unwell and gloomy. She lived as best she could *alla giornata,* without planning anything, 'taking each day as it came.'

On 15th May Mary heard that Byron had died from a fever in Greece. 'Can I forget his attentions & consolations to me during my deepest misery? Never. Beauty sat on his countenance and power beamed from his eye.' At his funeral in London Byron's coffin is supposed to have been followed by the empty carriages of those lords who were determined to avoid their scandalous fellow peer at all costs – even in death! His loss was another blow for Mary. 'Why am I doomed to live on seeing all expire before me? God grant I may die young.'

Chapter 19

Mary Shelley, now twenty-seven years old, still looked young and attractive, with golden hair, marble-white shoulders and those pretty sideways glances. She was so attractive, in fact, that many of her friends expected her to marry again. And over the next few years a number of men proposed marriage.

The first was John Howard Payne with whom she had a long friendship. When Payne was first introduced to her, he was so afraid of falling in love with Mary that he avoided her. Eventually he gave in and started taking her to see every play, opera and concert in London that she wanted to see. But when he proposed marriage Mary turned him down. She told him that she could only ever marry a man endowed with *Shelley's* rare quality of genius! It may be that there was someone out there of his calibre but if so she had not met him yet.

The American writer Washington Irving was one

such possibility. Amongst other accomplishments, he had written a life of Christopher Columbus. She was keen to develop a close friendship with him, but when he proposed to her she also turned him down.

Finally there was Trelawny who had regaled her with adventure stories when she had been living in Pisa. But she told him that 'My name will *never* be Trelawny... Mary Shelley will *never* be yours.' She wanted always to be 'Signora Shelley.' That was the 'pretty' name that she wanted written on her tomb.

On 21st June 1824 Mary decided to move out of London to Kentish Town. There Percy would be able to romp around on the wooded paths and gentle hills while she continued writing *The Last Man*. But she was miserable, short of money and found it difficult to write. When *The Last Man* was published in 1826 she was only paid £300 for it, compared with £400 for *Valperga*. And the reviews were awful, one critic calling it an 'elaborate piece of gloomy folly,' another pointing out anachronisms. Other critics talked about her godlessness. Over all, the reviews so demoralised her that she could not begin work on another novel for a year and a half.

It did not help to discover that Claire had betrayed her, gossiping about how bad Mary had been as a wife. In her Journal on 13th July Mary wrote: 'My friend has proved false and treacherous…! For four years I was devoted to her, and I earned only ingratitude.' Later that year, when she returned to live in Portman Square, she wrote to Claire: 'When I first heard that you did not love me – every hope of my life deserted me – the depression I sunk under, and to which I am now a prey, undermines my health – How many, many hours this dreary winter, I have paced my solitary room driven nearly to madness.' Friends noticed how sad she looked when she thought that nobody was watching her.

There was one ray of hope. Shelley's poems were selling well and he was becoming famous. But even this was spoilt by Shelley's father, Sir Timothy, wanting to keep control of his son's work. If any more copies were sold, or if Mary should publish a biography of Shelley during Sir Timothy's lifetime, he threatened to cut off his grandson's allowance. For Mary, who already had money problems, and was borrowing from Hogg and from Claire, this added worry was one she could well have done without.

Chapter 20

At the end of October 1827 Mary could have left London behind and chosen to begin a new life in the U.S.A. Her friend Fanny Trollope was sailing out there with her French lover and offered Mary the opportunity to travel with them. For a while she seriously considered this but in the end she said no: she needed to look after her son. Percy was now eight years old and needed plenty of attention. He had no social graces whatsoever; he was reluctant to take exercise and as a result had started to get fat. Shy and sensitive, he tended to avoid company and was terrified of girls. Mary thought that moving school might help him, and in April 1828 he started at Mr Slater's private school in Kensington. She hoped, before long, to send him to a better school, but for that to happen Sir Timothy would have to increase his allowance, and there was precious little chance of that happening.

With Percy at school, Mary was free to travel to Paris to meet her friends 'Mr and Mrs Douglas.' Really they were not Mr and Mrs Douglas at all but Maria Dods (Mary called her 'Doddy') and Isabel Robinson. Maria, who wrote books under the pseudonym David Lyndsay, had very short cropped hair and always looked and dressed much more like a man than a woman. The year before Mary had helped obtain passports for them both so they could leave England and live together in Paris, as they were now doing, as a married couple.

Parisian company was very agreeable and she went on to make new acquaintances, including the young poet Prosper Mérimé who had wounded his arm in a duel with his last mistress's husband. Mérimé was later to achieve fame as the author of the story on which the opera *Carmen* is based.

Mary loved Paris. She thought the city was beautiful and the weather was 'divine,' the air so much clearer than in smoky London. She spent most days outside, beneath the fresh green chestnut trees of the Tuileries gardens. But in spite of the good weather and pure air she went down with a fever. At first she thought she might have chicken pox. However, it turned out to be much more severe – smallpox. When Mary returned to England her father was shocked by her appearance. Her face was peppered with smallpox marks and her hair was in such a terrible state that she had to keep it clipped back. For a while she thought she might lose it all.

That summer, for the sake of her health, she decided to go with Percy to the seaside resort of Hastings in Sussex. How she looked forward to seeing something white rather than red when she looked in the mirror. To think that her face had been famous for its fair complexion. Trelawny had once commented how she 'lights up very well at night,' and 'shows to advantage in society.' But she knew it would take months to lose every trace of the blemishes on her face. She felt so ugly that she did not wish even to see her friends.

Chapter 21

From Hastings Mary returned to London and used her time to complete a historical romance entitled *The Fortunes of Perkin Warbeck,* for which she had been paid £150. Unfortunately, just before her novel came out on 13th May 1830 another novel about Perkin Warbeck was published. Some critics said that Mary's story was too gloomy and dull. In any event, it did not sell well.

The longer and lighter spring days began to lift her spirits. She started to go out again: 'I have begun a new kind of life somewhat – going a little into society – and forming a variety of acquaintances.' These friends knew little about her notorious past. One of these, Frances Wright, wanted Mary to come with her to the U.S.A. and join a movement to abolish slavery. But Mary needed to stay in England with Percy. In any case, she had friends in London now. She would love to have visited them more often, but the fares charged by the drivers of hansom cabs were so expensive. If only she had a carriage of her own.

Desperate for money, she offered the publishers John Murray suggestions for books – anything from 'The Conquests of Mexico and Peru' to the 'Lives of Celebrated Women.' They turned down all her proposals, probably suspicious of her claims to be able to write about such a wide range of subjects. As a stop-gap measure, she started to contribute essays on Italian, French and Spanish writers to an encyclopaedia. In the longer term she was planning another novel, a mystery called *Lodore.*

By that summer she had managed to save enough money to take Percy seabathing in Sandgate, near Folkestone, Kent. He was growing more and more like Shelley to look at but, unlike Shelley, was still very ill at ease with other people. If only she could introduce him to a nice girl – not that he was likely to meet one in Sandgate, where Mary 'never found so great a dearth of female beauty.'

Percy was now sixteen, he was too old to go to Mr Slater's school any longer, and needed to be sent to public school before going to Cambridge University. She chose Harrow School for him, and to save money in 1833 they moved to Harrow. That way he could be a day scholar and Mary could avoid expensive accommodation fees. But the other boys teased him about living at home; and when he lost some of his clothes in a fire at the school this caused further financial hardship for Mary. She was also dreadfully lonely there. 'Loneliness has been the curse of my life,' she wrote. 'What should I have done if my imagination had not been my companion?'

Disaster followed disaster. In the following year, 1834, forty-four pages of her new novel, *Lodore,* were lost. Either the printer or the Post Office was to blame. It was never found, and Mary had not kept a copy. In the end she had to rewrite it. Fortunately, *Lodore*, a high society mystery set partly in Essex and partly in Illinois U.S.A., turned out to be her most successful book since *Frankenstein*. When it sold over seven hundred copies the publisher, Charles Ollier, paid her a bonus.

By this time her father was beginning to show his age. He was unwilling to travel and would not even consider making the short journey to see Mary and Percy in Harrow. So, to be closer to him in the spring of 1836 Mary returned to London and moved into lodgings at Regent's Park. Two weeks later her father went down with a bad cough that turned into a fever. On 7th April he died. He was seventy-nine. Mary wrote 'I have lost my dear darling father.' She had him buried, as he had wished, by the side of her dear mother, his first love, in Old St Pancras Churchyard.

Mary vowed to write an account of her father's life. She would give the profits to support Mrs Godwin who had been left penniless. The proceeds from the publication of a new novel, as well as those arising from the sale of her father's library would also go to help 'poor Mrs G.' – that 'odious' and 'filthy' woman of her youth.

Chapter 22

Summer 1840

Percy would soon begin his final year at Cambridge University. Although he had had a brief romance there with a girl called Gertrude, he had no girl friend, no prospect of marriage. He would soon be twenty-one.

Mary was now forty-two and had been a widow for almost half her life. She was still attractive and compliments about her good looks continued to be paid to her. But she was starting to suffer more and more frequent bouts of ill health.

Travel always did wonders for Mary Shelley, and in June 1840 she had her chance to travel again. Percy and two of his friends from Cambridge had decided to spend their summer holiday on the shores of Lake Como, revising for their finals. They asked Mary to accompany them, and she gladly agreed. 'I was shown our way on the map,' wrote Mary, 'Metz to Treves;

then down the Moselle… to Coblentz; up the Rhine to Mayence; Frankfort, and the line South through Heidelberg, Baden Baden, Freyburg, Schaffhausen, Zurich, the Splugen, Chiavenna, to the Lake of Como.'

'Can it, indeed, be true, that I am about to revisit Italy?' she asked herself. 'How many years are gone since I quitted that country! There I left the mortal remains of those beloved – my husband and my children, whose loss changed my whole existence…'

But might Italy again prove fatal for her?

Taking her maid with her, Mary and her 'merry party of light-hearted youngsters' travelled to Paris, where they marvelled at the Place de la Concorde with its sparkling fountains and exotic lanterns, but complained at the lack of pavements and the hackney cabs that sped round corners and almost ran them over. After a week in Paris they boarded a stagecoach called a *diligence* to Germany, a land where people seemed to love fried potatoes, and horses ate more bread than horses anywhere she had seen. The hills grew higher and steeper and were crowned by ruined towers and castles, spires and abbeys. They were joined by two other Cambridge University students, and when they needed to sail down a difficult stretch of the Rhine, it was useful to have these lads with them because they were used to rowing at college.

Baden-Baden, then Switzerland. They crossed a mountain – 'dim mists, chilling blasts, and driving snow added to its grandeur.' At the top lay the border with Italy:

> 'All Italian travellers know what it is, after toiling up the bleak, bare, northern, Swiss side of an Alp, to descend towards ever-vernal Italy – with its pine forests, chestnut groves, woody ravines and waterfalls. Clothed in radiance, and gifted with plenty, Italy opened upon us.'

Paradise. Mary was happier than she had been for many years.

By mid July they had reached Lake Como where they stayed in the *Albergo Grande.* Mary set up her embroidery-frame, books and desk in a nook of the large room. Each morning they all worked. In the afternoons Percy would go off inspecting boats and soon found a small boat to his liking. 'In shape it is something of a sea boat, and it has a keel, and a tiny sail; but it is too small to convey a feeling of safety.' Mary looked at it and shuddered. His interest in yachting and swimming terrified her after what had happened to his father.

After a month they exchanged the lake and its

mountains for the plains of Bergamo where a great fair was in progress. They had been warned that the inns at Bergamo were notorious, and they found this only too true. Lizards climbed the bedroom walls, the waiters were 'unwashed, uncouth animals,' and the dinner had so much garlic in it that it was uneatable.

Towards the end of September Percy and his companions returned to England while Mary travelled on to Milan alone. On her return she stopped at Geneva for a break. Looking out of her hotel window she could see the wide lake and dark, high mountains. 'At length, I caught a glimpse of the scenes among which I had lived, when first I stepped out from childhood into life.' There stood the Villa Diodati where she had conceived the idea of Frankenstein's monster. 'Was I the same person who had lived there, the companion of the dead? For all were gone: even my young child… storm, and blight, and death, had passed over, and destroyed all.' That year, Mrs Godwin, who had been ill for some time, also died.

In the following summer, 1842, after a spell back in London and a visit to North Wales, Mary and Percy, together with an old Cambridge friend, sailed to Amsterdam. It was a journey full of problems: luggage got mislaid, a passport was lost, and two purses were stolen. From Amsterdam they travelled by train to Antwerp on one of the newly built railways.

At the spa town of Kissingen in Bavaria they found 'a crowd of invalids assembled *en masse*' – delicate-looking women and enormously fat men trying to thin down. They stayed at an inn where all they had in the way of washing facilities was a carafe of water to wash with and a pie dish to use as a basin. On the first morning there Mary got up at five o'clock to taste the spa waters, only to find that the Germans had been up since four! And when she sampled the water, the gas coming off it made her eyes weak and caused nervous spasms. The next part of the procedure was to bathe in hot water the colour of iron rust, which was poured into baths that were no bigger than coffins. At eight o'clock they had breakfast – another disappointment – butter, fruit, tea, coffee and milk were all banned, as they were all supposed to disagree with the spa water!

On the road out of Kissingen they met the Crown Prince of Bavaria, and in Dresden they went to the opera. From there to Prague, a picturesque city crowned with minarets, domes and spires. Then Italy – Venice, Florence and Rome, where they visited

Shelley's grave in the Protestant cemetery but never found the spot where her son William had been buried. Sorrento on the beautiful Amalfi coast was the furthest south they reached. Sadly, the view of the bay reminded her of the Bay of Lerici and the tragic events that had happened there.

In July 1843 they returned to England. Mary broke her journey in Paris, more out of duty than pleasure, to visit her step-sister Claire who had settled there. They had not seen each other for years and Claire had not answered her letters. Mary recalled that July dawn almost thirty years earlier when she had weakened and persuaded Shelley to take Claire (or rather Jane, as she was still known then) to Switzerland with them. How she had lived to regret that decision. For, over the years, Claire had been the cause of nothing but trouble. Deeply jealous of Mary's relationship with Shelley, she had become an irritating hanger-on, following them around Europe. Nothing had changed. She found Claire bitter, full of poison, and always ready to prick her conscience – about how hard she worked, how bad her health was, how Mary had been idly rambling around Europe when Mrs Godwin had been so ill two summers before. She was determined that Mary should never get her hands on some of her most precious possessions – keepsakes from Shelley, and William Godwin's writing desk, crammed with letters which her mother had inherited, and at her own death had passed on to Claire.

However, the visit to Paris did have its brighter side when Mary was introduced to a handsome young writer by the name of Ferdinando Gatteschi. He was a member of the 'Young Italy' movement that aimed to liberate Italy from Austria and create an independent republic. Mary had a weakness for clever young men, especially this almost penniless man who spoke with such passion about the liberation movement. So infatuated with him did she become that she borrowed money from Claire to help him. She also promised to find a publisher for his writing when she returned to England.

Gatteschi's only other source of income was from his employer, Count Martini, who kept him on at a pittance. Martini himself was short of money and, to raise funds, was keen to sell a very famous painting by Titian. The painting in question, 'Adulteress Brought Before Christ,' was then in Milan but he had an engraving of it which he showed her. Mary realised that if it could be sold she would not merely be helping Gatteschi but would probably gain something for herself besides. So she took the initiative of contacting the new National Gallery in London on Martini's behalf. The Gallery was very interested and Mary invited Martini to London as her guest in February 1844. But when the picture arrived it was quickly identified by the Gallery as a fake. That possible source of income had, after all, come to nothing, and Count Martini returned to Paris. As for Gatteschi, Mary's infatuation with him remained as strong as ever, and she continued to send him money.

By this time Mary had begun to write up an account of her travels around Europe. She only managed it in the mornings. By midday she would have to stop as her eyes would become sore. The result, *Rambles in Germany and Italy*, was to be her last major work. Although it turned out to be one of her most favourably reviewed books, Mary herself described it as 'a wretched piece of work, written much of it in a state of pain that makes me look at its pages as if written in a dream.'

Chapter 23

Percy continued to worry her. He had graduated from Cambridge over three years ago and was now twenty-five years old, short and becoming stout, with a round face and fair hair. At one time Mary had hoped that he would be her shining star, perhaps a great poet, but she had become reconciled to the idea that he would most probably study law. In November 1845 he was admitted to the Middle Temple, one of the four Inns of Court responsible for training student barristers.

Since 'coming of age' he had been receiving an allowance of four hundred pounds a year from the Shelley estate. Mary hoped that he would now meet that 'nice girl' and settle down. But his laziness and peculiar behaviour suggested that this was most unlikely to happen. He was still very withdrawn and took long walks on his own at night. Neither in Florence nor in Rome had he shown the least bit of interest in the paintings, and had spent most of his time fooling about playing his trumpet or his flute. Unlike Mary, who would love to have settled in Italy, Percy was forever wishing he was back home in England where a model of a 'Flying Machine' was on display and he could go to exciting lectures about aerial navigation.

They now had the opportunity of moving into the Shelley home at Field Place, near Horsham in Sussex. Lady Shelley was vacating the property and had invited Mary to have a look at it. But Mary was less interested in the property than in buying Lady Shelley's carriage – as she had never owned one herself. As for the house, she found it a desperately dull place in a dilapidated state. Percy would either vegetate there, 'or be forced from sheer ennui to make love to the dairy maid.' Instead they rented a house close to the Thames at Putney. Percy joined the Royal Thames Yacht Club – and, needless to say, bought another boat! With their new wealth they could even buy presents for their friends. One of their closest friends, Leigh Hunt, whose writing was not selling, was facing poverty. Without the support of Shelley and Byron he needed help, so Mary made an arrangement to pay him £120 a year for the rest of his life.

In December 1845 they could afford to move to 24 Chester Square, a four storey house in the Pimlico area of London. After a lifetime of moving house, this was the first home Mary had ever owned. She intended to use the house to introduce Percy to society. At present he was completely hopeless in company, he could not think fast and tended to mumble when asked questions. It caused a particular problem when, as a new baronet (or, more exactly, third baronet of Castle Goring), he was presented to Queen Victoria and Prince Albert. He went to the ceremony alone and stood awkwardly by himself in a corner.

So, imagine Mary's surprise when Percy announced in 1846 that he intended to stand for Parliament and become M.P. for Horsham at the next election. As it turned out, he quickly realised that the election contest would be expensive and gave up the idea, deciding instead to spend money on improving Field Place – and buying a new yacht!

If only he would show as much interest in girls, thought Mary. Percy was still very shy and tended to shut himself away from them. What if he should fall in love with the first one who showed any interest in him – no matter how unsuitable? Better that she put him in touch with 'eligible' ones from intellectual circles. Her task would not be easy.

But in 1847, while staying at the house of a mutual friend, Mary and Percy were introduced to a Mrs Jane Gibson St John, a small plump widow, one year younger than Percy. She had been married to Charles St John and had inherited a personal fortune on his death in 1844. Next Spring Mary asked her to stay with them in Chester Square. She was delighted with Jane, so affectionate and bubbling with energy. Although no beauty, nor an intellectual, she surely had to be 'the best and sweetest thing in the world.' What a match for her son. Jane would make a perferct wife.

On 24th March Percy and Jane became engaged and on 22nd June 1848 they got married in St George's Church, Hanover Square, London. They honey-mooned close to Wordsworth's home in the Lake District before returning to Field Place. There they lived quietly with Mary, looking after the garden and farm, the dogs and the birds. Their calm was only broken when Claire came to see them. 'She has been the bane of my life ever since I was two,' Mary told her daughter-in-law. After one outburst Mary asked her to leave and not come back.

Field Place was a draughty and damp house, and they soon decided to move. They took a short holiday enjoying the hot sunshine of Nice, and when they returned they went to live in Dorset. The spot Percy and Jane chose was Boscombe Manor, near Bournemouth – a one hundred and ninety-five acre estate, shielded by tall pine trees. Meanwhile, Mary decided to move back to her house in Chester Square, London.

Chapter 24

By this time Mary had become ill. She had already had a physician relieve pressure on her spinal nerves. Now she complained of pressure on the brain. Her eyes had become weak and inflamed. She started to suffer dizzy spells and reported 'swimming' sensations in her head. As time passed the headaches grew worse, her left arm lost all feeling and her left leg went into tremors. It was all a mystery. Percy wrote 'Her illness puzzled the doctors so long, and presented so many different appearances that they could not make out what was the matter with her.'

But if the causes of her illness were unknown, the *effects* had a catastrophic effect on the plans she had set herself. Although she now had all the necessary source material at her fingertips – including some early love letters between Shelley and herself – she was unable to get down to her all important biography. She had supported herself for almost thirty years through her writing – as a novelist, editor, critic, travel and short story writer, and biographer – but she could do so no longer.

Meanwhile, Shelley's cousin, Thomas Medwin, was threatening to produce a 'warts and all' life of Shelley which would expose incidents capable of causing a sensation – such as his treatment of Harriet and the custody battle for his children. His price for not publishing it was £250. Mary refused to pay, which was just as well because when the book was published it caused little stir.

When Ferdinando Gatteschi reappeared on the scene it did not help matters. She had once been infatuated with him and had written him love letters but had turned down his offer of marriage. Gatteschi had since moved on to another woman, Lady Sussex Lennox. However he still felt badly treated by Mary, and believed she had led him on. To get revenge on her he threatened to publish Mary's love letters.

With all these worries Mary was in need of a holiday. In September 1849 Mary, Percy and Jane went on a tour of France and Italy. From Lake Como on 26 May 1850 she wrote to her childhood friend from Dundee, Isabella Baxter (now Isabella Booth) but to her always 'Izy.' She talked about how difficult it was for her to walk, her nervous spasms, how she had grown old. She asked after her friend's health, also that of her daughter and her nine grandchildren, and said how she looked forward to hearing from her. It was to be one of the last letters that she wrote.

Mary returned from the tour no better. The dry, irritating air of Nice had done nothing to soothe her nerves at all. Doctors talked about 'nervous rheumatism' and 'neuralgia.' Her spine tingled, and even a short walk was an ordeal for her. Then her left leg started to become numb. One doctor recommended cod-liver oil, another had her sip wine, a third suggested a change of air – and, of course, a stay at the seaside. For the first time in her life she owned the carriage she had always wanted. It would have taken her to the sea. But unfortunately she no longer had the good health to enjoy a carriage. Her condition was finally diagnosed by Dr Richard Bright on 17th December 1850 – Mary was suffering from a brain tumour. The dreadful news was kept secret from Percy.

Towards the end of January 1851 Mary suffered a series of strokes. She knew that she was dying but was not afraid. She had lost this fear when she had almost died from her miscarriage in Italy.

Mary died on 1st February 1851. She was fifty-three years old. Her death certificate reads: 'Mary

Wollstonecraft Shelley, Female, 53 Years, Widow of Percy Bysshe Shelley Esq. Cause of death Disease of the brain Supposed Tumour in left hemisphere of long standing certified.'

Jane Shelley said that for three years Mary had been to her more than a mother, sister and a friend; she had been her daily and hourly companion. She called her the 'noblest of creatures,' 'totally unselfish,' and said how 'it was impossible for any living thing to approach her and not love her...'

Mary did not leave a will. But Percy said that one morning before she was very ill she had told him that she wanted her friend 'Izy' to have £50 per year.

She had always dreamed of being buried next to Shelley but the expense involved in transporting her body to Rome was too great. On the other hand, Percy and Jane could not have Mary buried in Old St Pancras Churchyard which was such a dreadful place. So they had the bodies of her mother and her father exhumed and taken down to Bournemouth near to where they lived, to be buried by Mary's side. That way Jane would be able to keep fresh flowers on her grave. In the next year or so they hoped to reunite the whole family by going on a pilgrimage to Rome and bringing home the urn with Shelley's ashes.

At first, the vicar of St Peter's Church in

Bournemouth, who had built the church largely at his own expense, refused to have the bodies of such a 'heretical trio' buried in his churchyard and locked the gates. But Lady Jane Shelley would have none of it. She led the two hearses to the cemetery gates and made it clear that she would wait there until she was allowed in. Eventually the vicar yielded and, under cover of darkness, the gravediggers set to work and the bodies were buried together in a large grave without a religious service. A memorial stone marked all their names and the titles of her parents' most famous books – but no mention was made at that time of Mary Shelley's *Frankenstein.* In 1854 Percy commissioned a monument in white marble, depicting Shelley's body, supported by Mary. He had intended that it be put in St Peter's Church but again the vicar refused, saying that it would take peoples' minds off the service and make the church too much of a tourist attraction. The monument was offered instead to the Priory Church in Christchurch which accepted it. It can still be seen today by the west door beneath the tower.

Percy and Jane were not fortunate enough to have children of their own. Instead they adopted Jane's niece, Florence Gibson, as their daughter. They spent the rest of their lives at Boscombe Manor, and right until his death in 1889 at the age of seventy Percy

continued to sail his yacht on the Solent.

But his mother, Mary Shelley, had been snatched away by death's grasp:

> A child of genius,
> A peeress, girt about with magic powers,
> That could at will evoke from her wild thought
> Spirits unearthly, monster-shaped, to strike
> Terror within us, and strange wonderments
> Renewing, realizing, once again,
> With daring fancy, on her thrilling page,
> The fabled story of Prometheus old.'
> [anon.]

For some time after his mother's death Percy could not bear to be in the house where she had died. Nor could he let anyone touch her things. But on the first anniversary of her death, Percy and Jane opened the desk by the side of Mary's bed. There was a lock of hair lying on top of Mary Shelley's Journal. They also found a sheet of paper that seemed to have been torn from a book of poems and made into an envelope, tied up with silk. Carefully they undid the knot. Inside was some powder. Both were aware of the story that Shelley's heart would not burn. Had Mary preserved his heart, the love of her life? Over the years had it disintegrated into what now lay before them? Perhaps Mary could not bear to part with what remained of her husband, it being impossible for her to repeat in reality what she had once achieved in fiction – the recreation of life in her immortal novel, *Frankenstein*.

Key dates in the life of Mary Shelley

1797	30 Aug. Mary was born in London 10 Sept. Her mother, Mary Wollstonecraft, dies
1801	21 Dec. Her father, William Godwin, marries Mary Clairmont
1805	William and Mary Godwin open a publishing company
1808	They publish Mary's poem, *Mounseer Nongtonpaw*
1811	Mary travels to Ramsgate for her health
1812	7 June Mary is sent to Dundee, Scotland, to live with the Baxters 11 Nov. On her return, Mary meets Shelley and his wife

1813	3 June Mary's second visit to Dundee
1814	28 July Mary elopes with Percy Shelley to France and Switzerland 13 Sept. The Shelleys return to London
1815	22 Feb. Mary's premature daughter, Clara, is born but lives only 11 days 4 Aug. The Shelleys move to Windsor
1816	'The year without a summer' 24 Jan. Mary's son, William, is born 3 May The Shelleys travel to Geneva 16 June Mary starts to write *Frankenstein* 9 Oct. Fanny Imlay commits suicide 10 Dec. Harriet Shelley commits suicide 30 Dec. Mary and Shelley marry in St Mildred's Church, London
1817	2 Sept. Mary's daughter, Clara Everina, is born 6 Nov. Mary publishes *History of a Six Weeks Tour*
1818	1 Jan. *Frankenstein* is published 11 Mar. The Shelleys leave for Italy 24 Sept. Clara Everina dies from a fever

1819 7 June William dies from malaria in Rome
17 June The Shelleys move to Leghorn
Aug. Mary starts writing *Mathilda*
2 Oct. The Shelleys move to Florence
12 Nov. Percy Florence Shelley is born

1820 26 Jan. The Shelleys arrive in Pisa
Nov. Shelley befriends Emilia Viviani

1821 19 Jan. Edward and Jane Williams arrive in Pisa

1822 30 Apr. The Shelleys and Claire move to *Casa Magni* in San Terenzo.
16 June Mary miscarries and almost dies
8 July Shelley drowns in a shipwreck
11 Sept. Mary moves to Genoa

1823 19 Feb. *Valperga* is published
29 July The play *Fate of Frankenstein* is performed
25 Aug. Mary returns to London with her son Percy

1824 19 Apr. Byron dies in Greece

1826 23 Jan. *The Last Man* is published

1827 24 July Mary helps forge passports

1830 13 May *The Fortunes of Perkin Warbeck* is published

1832 29 Sept. Percy Florence Shelley starts at Harrow School

1835 7 Apr. *Lodore* is published

1836 7 Apr. William Godwin dies

1837 Feb. *Falkner. A Novel* is published
10 Oct. Percy Shelley starts at Trinity College, Cambridge

1840-43 Mary travels in Europe

1841 17 June Mrs Godwin dies

1844 July *Rambles in Germany and Italy* is published

1848 22 June Percy Florence Shelley marries Jane St John

1850 Mary suffers nervous attacks and partial paralysis

1851 1 Feb. Mary dies from a brain tumour and is buried in Bournemouth

Brief biographical notes on the people in the story

Mary Shelley's family

William Godwin (1756-1836)

Mary Shelley's father who married Mary Wollstonecraft in 1797 and to whom *Frankenstein* is dedicated. English journalist, political philosopher and a prolific writer of novels, history and children's books. In *An Enquiry Concerning Political Justice* (1793) he called for the overthrow of monarchy and religion – gradually, not through violence. It sold over 4,000 copies and made him famous. He also wrote *Things as They Are: The Adventures of Caleb Williams* (1794), the first thriller ever to be written. With his second wife he published Charles and Mary Lamb's *Tales from Shakespeare.*

Mary Wollstonecraft (1759-97) Mary Shelley's

mother. Most famous for her book *Vindication of the Rights of Women* in which she described how women were kept in a state of 'ignorance and slavish dependence,' and how marriage was just 'legalised prostitution.' In her earlier pamphlet *Vindication of the Rights of Man* she had pointed out what she thought was wrong with society – including the slave trade and the way in which the poor were treated. She also wrote *Thoughts on the Education of Girls* in which she attacked traditional teaching methods and suggested that girls ought to be educated with boys. Her revolutionary ideas earned her the nickname 'hyena in petticoats.'

Mary Shelley's circle

Byron, George (1788-1824)
Anglo-Scottish poet, best known for his poems *Childe Harold's Pilgrimage* and *Don Juan* which he finished at Pisa. He is famous for his flamboyance, unpredictable temper, his numerous love affairs, and a limp that caused him lifelong suffering. Most of his life he lived abroad to escape criticism from British society about his scandalous lifestyle. He helped the Greeks fight for their independence against the Turks,

spending £4,000 of his own money to refit the Greek fleet. His daughter, Ada, helped Charles Babbage invent the computer.

Coleridge, Samuel Taylor (1772-1834)

English poet, critic and philosopher. He received an award for his *Ode on the slave trade* (1792) but is best known for his poems *The Rime of the Ancient Mariner* (which Mary Shelley mentions twice in *Frankenstein)* and *Kubla Khan.* He often visited the Godwins in London with his friend, William Wordsworth.

Hunt, Leigh (1784-1859)

English poet and writer. In 1813, when editor of the *Examiner* newspaper, he wrote an article attacking the Prince Regent and was given a two year prison sentence. He belonged to the Hampstead circle of writers – along with Percy Bysshe Shelley, Keats and Charles Lamb. In 1825 he went to Italy to set up a liberal magazine, and published a 'warts and all' biography of Byron. He ended his life in poverty.

Keats, John (1795-1821)

One of the main poets of the English Romantic movement, and a friend of Leigh Hunt. He wrote a series of odes, including *Ode on a Grecian Urn* and

Ode to a Nightingale. In 1820 his doctors recommended that he leave the cold airs of London and move to Italy. His early death inspired Shelley to write the poem *Adonais.*

Lamb, Charles (1775-1834)
English essayist who went to school with Samuel Taylor Coleridge. He is best known for his children's book *Tales from Shakespeare* which he wrote with his sister, Mary Lamb, and which the Godwins published.

Polidori, John (1795-1821)
Italian-English physician and writer. In 1816 he became Lord Byron's personal physician and accompanied him on a trip through Europe. He was present with the Shelleys and Byron at the ghost story competition at the Villa Diodati in Geneva, Switzerland. Polidori wrote *The Vampyre,* the first vampire story published in English. His vampire, who preys upon high society, is based not on a beast but on Byron. Depressed and in debt, he probably committed suicide by taking prussic acid.

Trelawny, Edward (1792-1881)
English adventurer and author. In 1821 he became a companion of the Shelleys and Byron in Italy. In 1822

he helped to recover and cremate the bodies of Shelley and Edward Williams drowned off Viareggio. Trelawny arranged for Shelley's ashes to be buried in the Protestant Cemetery, Rome, and he provided the money for Mary Shelley to be able to return to England.

Wordsworth, William (1770-1850)
A major English Romantic poet who lived much of his life at Ambleside in the Lake District. In his writing he explores unconscious impulses and desires. He defined poetry as 'the spontaneous overflow of powerful feelings.' One of his most famous poems is *Daffodils* (1804).

The scientists who influenced her

Darwin, Erasmus (1731-1802)
English Physician, natural philosopher, physiologist, inventor and poet. He was one of the founder members of the Lunar Society, a discussion group of inventors and natural philosophers who met in Birmingham. He invented a carriage that would not tip over, a speaking machine, a canal lift for barges and a tiny artificial bird. Darwin was a friend of William

Godwin, and, like him, opposed the slave trade and supported the American and French Revolutions. In his poem *The Origin of Society* he traced the progression of life from micro-organisms to civilized society. His experiments in galvanism (named after Luigi Galvani, below) helped inspire Mary Shelley to write *Frankenstein.*

Galvani, Luigi (1737-98)
Italian physician and physicist who experimented with frogs and showed that electricity could make their muscles twitch. Mary Shelley had just read a report of his investigations in the summer that she began work on *Frankenstein.*

Where to find out more about Mary Shelley

Useful books

Moon in eclipse: a life of Mary Shelley by J. Dunn (Weidenfeld and Nicolson, 1978)

Mary Shelley – Her Life, her fiction, her monsters by Anne K. Mellor (Routledge, 1989)

Mary Shelley by Muriel Spark (Cardinal, 1989)

Mary Shelley – Romance and Reality by Emily W. Sunstein (The Johns Hopkins University Press, 1991)

Selected Letters of Mary Wollstonecraft Shelley edited by Betty T. Bennett (The Johns Hopkins University Press, 1995)

Mary Shelley, Frankenstein's Creator by Joan Nichols (Conari Press, 1998)

Mary Shelley by Miranda Seymour (Picador, 2000)

A Mary Shelley Encyclopaedia by Lucy Morrison and Staci L. Stone (Greenwood Press, 2003)

The man who wrote Frankenstein by John Lauritsen (Pagan Press, 2007)

The Original Frankenstein edited by Charles E. Robinson (Bodleian Library, 2008)

Useful websites

http://en.wikipedia.org/wiki/Mary_Shelley

www.kirjasto.sci.fi/mshelley.htm

http://www.bibliomania.com/0/0/43/frameset.html

http://www.online-literature.com/shelley_mary/

Films

Gothic (1986) directed by Ken Russell and starring Gabriel Byrne as Lord Byron, Julian Sands as Percy Bysshe Shelley, Natasha Richardson as Mary Shelley and Timothy Spall as Dr Polidori

Haunted Summer (1988) starring Philip Anglim, Laura Dern, Alice Krige, Eric Stoltz and Alex Winter

Some examples of the many films about Frankenstein

Frankenstein, Edison Film Company, 1910 (USA)

Frankenstein, Universal, 1931 (USA) Boris Karloff

The Bride of Frankenstein, Universal, 1935 (USA) Boris Karloff

The Ghost of Frankenstein, Universal, 1942 (USA)

Frankenstein Meets the Wolf Man, Universal, 1943 (USA)

Abbot and Costello Meet Frankenstein, Universal-International, 1948 (USA)

The Curse of Frankenstein, Hammer Films, 1957 (UK) Peter Cushing

I Was a Teenage Frankenstein, American International Pictures, 1957 (USA)

Frankenstein's Daughter, Astor Pictures/Layton Film Productions, 1958 (USA)

The Revenge of Frankenstein, Hammer Films, 1958 (UK) Peter Cushing

The Evil of Frankenstein, Hammer Films, 1964 (UK) Peter Cushing

Frankenstein Meets the Space Monster, Vernon Films/Seneca/Futurama Entertainment, 1965 (USA)

Jesse James Meets Frankenstein's Daughter, Embassy Pictures/Circle, 1965 (USA)

Frankenstein Created Woman, Hammer Films, 1966 (UK) Peter Cushing

Fearless Frank, American International Pictures, 1967 (USA)

Dr. Frankenstein on Campus, Astral Films/Agincourt, 1970 (Canada)

Dracula vs. Frankenstein, Independent-International Pictures, 1970 (USA)

The Horror of Frankenstein, Hammer, 1970 (UK)

Dracula Prisoner of Frankenstein, Fenix Films *et al.*, 1972 (Spain, France, Lichtenstein, and Portugal)

Frankenstein and the Monster from Hell, Hammer, 1973 (UK) Peter Cushing

Young Frankenstein / Frankenstein Junior, Twentieth-Century Fox, 1974 (USA) Mel Brooks

The Rocky Horror Picture Show, Twentieth-Century Fox, 1975 (UK)

Frankenweenie, Walt Disney Productions, 1984 (USA)

Frankenstein General Hospital, New Star Entertainment, 1988 (USA)

Frankenstein's Baby, BBC-TV, 1990 (UK)

Frankenstein: The College Years, FNM Films, 1991 (USA)

Mary Shelley's Frankenstein, America Zoetrope/TriStar Pictures, 1994 (UK and USA) Directed by Kenneth Branagh, starring Robert De Niro, Kenneth Branagh, Helena Bonham-Carter, John Cleese

Dramatisations of *Frankenstein* during Mary Shelley's lifetime

Frankenstein; ou, Le Prométhée moderne, never performed, (Aug. 1821)

Presumption; or, The Fate of Frankenstein by Richard Brinsley Peake, Lyceum Theatre, London (July 1823) Both Thomas Cooke, who played the monster in *Presumption*, and Boris Karloff who did so a century later, progressed to playing Dr Frankenstein

Frankenstein, or The Danger of Presumption, Royalty Theatre, London (1823)

Frankenstein; or, The Demon of Switzerland by Henry M. Milner, Royal Coburg Theatre London (Aug. 1823)

Humgumption; or, Dr Frankenstein and the Hobgoblin of Hoxton, New Surrey Theatre (Sept 1823)

Presumption and the Blue Demon, Davis's Royal Amphitheatre (Sept. 1823)

Another Piece of Presumption by Richard Brinsley Peake, Adelphi Theatre (Oct. 1823)

Frank-in-Steam; or, The Modern Promise to Pay Olympic Theatre (Dec. 1824)

Le Monstre et le magician by Jean Toussaint Merle and Antoine Nicolas Béraud, Théâtre de la Porte Saint-Martin, Paris (June 1826)

The Man and the Monster; or, The Fate of Frankenstein by Henry M. Milner. Royal Coburg Theatre (July 1826)

Les Filets du Vulcain; ou, Le Vénus de Neuilly by Nicolas razier, Guillaume Dumersan and Gabriel-Jules-Joseph de Laurien, Théâtre des Variétés (June 1826)

Le petit monstre et l'escamoteur by Jules-Henri Vernoy de Saint-Georges and Antoine-Jean-Baptiste Simonnin, Théâtre de la Gaîeté, Paris (July 1826)

La Pêche de Vulcain; ou, l'île des fleuves by Claude-Louis-Marie de Rochefort-Luçay, Esperance-Hippolyte Lassagne and Mathurin-Joseph Brisset, Théâtre du Vaudeville, Paris (July 1826)

Le Présomteueux, Théâtre de M. Comte (July 1826)

Les Filets de Vulcain; ou, le lendemain d'un succès by P. Carmouche, Théâtre de la Porte Saint-Martin, Paris (July 1826)

Le Monstre et le physician, Théâtre de M. Comte, Paris (Aug. 1826)

The Monster and Magician; *or, The Fate of Frankenstein* by John Kerr, New Royal West London Theatre (Oct. 1826)

Frankenstein; or, The Model Man by William and Robert Brough, Adelphi Theatre, London (Dec. 1849)

What the critics said about *Frankenstein*

'Our taste and our judgement alike revolt at this kind of writing,'
(*The Quarterly Review*, January 1818)

'[Mary Shelley should] rather study the established order of nature as it appears, both in the world of matter and of mind, than continue to revolt our feelings by hazardous innovations...'
(*The Edinburgh Magazine and Literary Miscellany,* March 1818)

'This work... has, as well as originality, extreme interest to recommend it, and an easy, yet energetic style...'
(*The Belle Assemblée, or Bell's Court and Fashionable Magazine,* March 1818).

'An uncouth story, in the taste of the German novelists... setting probability at defiance, and leading to no conclusion either moral or philosophical.'
(*Monthly Review*, March 1818)

'we shall...dismiss the novel without further comment.' (*The British Critic*, 9 April 1818)

'This novel is a feeble imitation of one that was very popular in its day – the St. Leon of Mr. Godwin. It exhibits many characteristics of the school whence it proceeds; and occasionally puts forth indications of talent; but we have been very much disappointed in the perusal of it, from our expectations having been raised too high beforehand by injudicious praises.'
(*The Literary Panorama and National Register*, June 1818)

'the author seems to us to disclose uncommon powers of poetic imagination... original genius...plain and forcible English.' (Sir Walter Scott, 1818)

'This is, perhaps, the foulest Toadstool that has yet sprung up from the reeking dunghill of present times.' (William Beckford, 1818)

'[The novel contains] passages which appal the mind and make the fresh creep.... a tissue of horrible and disgusting absurdity.'
(John Wilson Croker, 1819)

Acknowledgements

I would like to thank Aimée Brooks, Emma Forge, Lucy Porter and Diana Williams for their helpful comments on earlier drafts of this book.